JUST IN TIME!

COMMUNION SERVICES

Robin Knowles Wallace

Abingdon Press
Nashville

LIBRARY
ROSE CITY PARK
UNITED METHODIST CHURCH
5830 N.E. ALAMEDA
PORTLAND, ORE. 97213

JUST IN TIME!
COMMUNION SERVICES

Copyright 2006 by Abingdon Press

All rights reserved.
Prayers, litanies, and other worship resources in this book, except as noted, may be reproduced by local church congregations, provided the following credit line and copyright notice appear on all copies: From *Communion Services* by Robin Knowles Wallace. Copyright © 2006 by Abingdon Press. Reproduced by permission. No other part of this work may be reproduced or transmitted in any form or by any means, electronic or mechanical, including photocopying and recording, or by any information storage or retrieval system, except as may be expressly permitted by the 1976 Copyright Act or in writing from the publisher. Requests for permission should be addressed to Abingdon Press, P.O. Box 801, 201 Eighth Avenue South, Nashville, TN 37202-0801 or permissions@abingdonpress.com.

This book is printed on acid-free paper.

Library of Congress Cataloging-in-Publication Data

Wallace, Robin Knowles.
    Communion services / Robin Knowles Wallace.
       p. cm. (Just in time!)
    Includes bibliographical references.
    ISBN 0-687-49836-8 (bdg.: adhesive : alk. paper)
    1. Lord's Supper (Liturgy) I. Title. II. Series (Nashville, Tenn)
    BV825.5.W35 2006
    264'.36--dc22

                                                                    2005022067

All scripture quotations unless noted otherwise are taken from the *New Revised Standard Version of the Bible,* copyright 1989 by the Division of Christian Education of the National Council of the Churches of Christ in the United States of America. Used by permission. All rights reserved.

06 07 08 09 10 11 12 13 14 15—10 9 8 7 6 5 4 3 2 1
MANUFACTURED IN THE UNITED STATES OF AMERICA

With thanks to the Triune God for the gift of
Communion and to my mother and father, Carolyn
and Millard Knowles, who first taught me to uncover
its riches

CONTENTS

Contents

Contents

How to Use This Book

The Communion meal is one of two distinguishing practices of Christianity, along with Baptism. Many congregations are including Communion more often in their worship than in previous years. This book is meant both as an introduction to the practice of Communion, and as a collection of Communion prayers and resources for worship, which may be used by various Protestant denominations. The prayers are *ready to use*. They also provide options for use in various situations and in worship services with different scripture and themes.

Chapter one includes information on Communion elements, vessels, and methods; and four possible orders for the Communion portion of a worship service, ranging from the most traditional and longest to the simplest outline.

Chapter two focuses on prayers and resources for specific seasons and holy days in the church year, from Advent through Thanksgiving. It also includes resources for use during the Ordinary Time of the church year.

In chapter three you will find prayers for events in the life of individuals and churches, including: confirmation, services of commissioning, camps, hospitals, shut-ins, beginning of the school year, weddings, and funerals. Finally, chapter four contains information on resources for further study.

It is possible to take the various elements from the introductory chapter and the prayers that follow in this book and develop a wide variety of services. The Great Thanksgiving prayers are all ready to use as written. You may also adapt them, using the resource section that follows many of the prayers. These resources include suggestions for congregational songs and responses, spoken table dismissals, and other material. The important thing is to approach your planning and the service reverently, in thanksgiving for this gift of our Creator to us—the life, death, and resurrection of Jesus Christ—that by the power of the Holy Spirit we might be in communion with the holy Trinity.

In this book, as in many other worship books, the words in prayers, shown in bold print, are meant to be said in unison by the whole congregation. Words in regular print are meant to be said by one person, the presider, or pastor. Directions are occasionally given in italic print. Scripture quotations are taken from the *New Revised Standard Version of the Bible*. All prayers may be reproduced for bulletins or overheads, provided the following credit line and copyright notice appear on each copy: From *Communion Services* by Robin Knowles Wallace. Copyright © 2006 by Abingdon Press. Reproduced by permission.

CHAPTER ONE

ABOUT COMMUNION

Whether you think of it as a sacrament or an ordinance, Communion is an essential part of the life of the worshiping community, given by Jesus to his followers at the Last Supper. Along with Baptism, Communion is one of the marks of Christianity, part of what defines us as Christian and draws us together as church. The Scriptures that record Jesus' words around the bread and cup are often called the Words of Institution, found in 1 Corinthians 11:23-25, Matthew 26:26-29, Mark 14:22-25, and Luke 22:14-20.

Churches that call Communion a sacrament mean that they understand it as a means or channel for God's grace to come to us, particularly as Jesus Christ is made present spiritually with us in the service. Churches that call Communion an ordinance mean that they understand it as something Jesus commanded us to do when he said "Do this in remembrance of me."

Communion has several names: Holy Communion, Eucharist, the Lord's Supper, and Breaking of the Bread. *Breaking of the Bread* is the term used in the Acts of the Apostles as a reminder of the early church and their incorporation of this holy meal on a weekly basis. *The Lord's Supper* reminds us that this is Christ's table, instituted by him for our sake, a gift through Jesus for all times. *Eucharist* may seem more formal, but it comes from the Greek word for giving thanks, and reminds us of all the blessings God has given us. *Holy Communion* reminds us that we commune both with God and with one another at the table, drawing forgiveness and strength from God, and becoming one body with other Christians to go forth in ministry.

Whatever you call it, and whether you see it as sacrament or ordinance, Communion has several essentials. In prayer, we thank God for all the good things given to us and for God's faithfulness in keeping promises. We remember the life, death, and resurrection of Jesus Christ. The Holy Spirit is present to bring us into the presence of God and to help us remember Jesus. The congregation is invited to the table, and to fellowship with both God and each other. Bread and wine or juice are the elements that we use to remember Jesus. Communion works in us to strengthen us for Christian living. It is a reminder to us that we are baptized, forgiven, and called to live new lives in Christ. These essentials of Communion historically include four actions:

Taking the elements: also called the Offertory

Blessing the elements: called the Great Thanksgiving, Communion Prayer, or Prayer of Consecration

Breaking the bread: called the Fraction

Giving the elements: called the Distribution

THE COMMUNION ELEMENTS

Bread and drink are the traditional elements of Communion. Christians follow the Jewish tradition of understanding that God can use simple, everyday things to remind us of God's promise and presence. The Synoptic Gospels (Matthew, Mark, and Luke) tell us that Jesus' last meal with his disciples before his death was the Passover meal, celebrating the Hebrew people's exodus from oppression and slavery into the Promised Land. Bread and wine were part of that Passover meal, but Jesus gave them new meaning when he said that the bread was his body broken for us, and that the wine was his blood given for the forgiveness of our sins. The Gospel of John suggests that Jesus was crucified on the day when the lambs were slaughtered for the Passover meal (John 19:31), so the Last Supper would have been before the traditional

Passover meal (John 13:1). But John's Gospel also has an important chapter with the sayings about Jesus as the bread of life (John 6:22-59), which helps us understand more deeply what Jesus says in the other Gospels about the bread and his body.

History of Communion Elements

We know from the Acts of the Apostles that the early church celebrated Communion as part of a larger fellowship meal. Early manuscripts giving directions for Communion mention the giving of bread and drinking from the cup, sometimes three in number: water to remember our washing in Baptism, milk and honey to remember the Promised Land, and wine as a remembrance of Jesus' blood and the new covenant. These early manuscripts also contain blessings for other foods such as olives and cheese, which would be shared with the poor.

Within the first four centuries of the church, however, Communion focused on bread and drink solely. As theology began to focus on how the bread and drink became the actual body and blood of Christ, the elements themselves came to be seen as more holy. This holiness was reflected by changes from daily bread to wafers that would not leave crumbs, and to withholding the cup from the congregation, so that no parts of the body and blood of Christ would be spilled.

Bread

Both leavened and unleavened bread have been used throughout history. Unleavened bread has been used to remind us that the God of Jesus is the God of the Passover and that we are freed from our slavery to sin. Leavened bread reminds us of everyday bread and of Jesus' parable that the kingdom of God is like yeast that a woman uses to bake bread (Luke 13:20-21). The catacomb drawings of early Communion services depict very large loaves that appear to be leavened bread. In the Middle Ages, as mentioned above, wafers became popular. Wafers are still used in many churches, in part because they are easily accessible and long lasting; for some people they represent this holy meal as they experienced it growing up.

Many churches are now going back to using everyday bread—unsliced leavened loaves. These loaves may be then broken, reminding us of Christ's sacrifice for us, after the Communion prayer. Whole loaves may then be broken into as many pieces as there are servers for intinction (see below) or into as many pieces needed to provide bread within reach of persons kneeling around the altar rail. In the past, the bread was sometimes cut into cubes, but these dry out quickly.

There are books and Web sites that have recipes for Communion bread. It is particularly nice to have someone in the congregation bake the bread for Communion, connecting the congregation and the meal more closely. Having a Sunday school class or youth group bake the bread at the church that morning adds the good smell of baking bread to the church building; but it is also appropriate to use various types of purchased, leavened white and wheat bread, particularly unsliced. Loaves may be round or oblong. Pita bread is also an acceptable option, as it is the common bread of the Middle East, the land of Jesus' birth. Real bread does make crumbs, but life is messy; yet God, through Jesus, is with us in it all.

When considering bread for Communion, do avoid nuts or seeds as they can choke or contain allergens. But simple, mild flavors can be used to vary the bread—dark bread for Lent, slightly sweetened bread for Advent or Easter, mild herbs in summer.

The Cup of Wine or Juice

Wine was the drink of festive and holy meals in Jesus' time and thus the natural drink of the Lord's Supper. Some wines of that time needed to have water added to be drinkable; this was later interpreted by Christians as the water and blood that flowed from Jesus' side when the soldier pierced it during the crucifixion (John 19:34). Because of its association with the blood of Christ, wine served during Communion has traditionally been red.

Like bread, wine was given in smaller and smaller amounts as history progressed; until in the Middle Ages congregations received just the bread, with only the priest also taking wine. The church of that time developed a theological understanding that both Jesus' body and blood were present in each element alone, so taking only the bread was considered sufficient. One of the important tenets of the Reformation was the restoration of the cup to the laity during Communion.

In the 1800s here in the United States, the Temperance movement led to concern for alcoholics, and the new process of pasteurization was applied to wine beginning in 1869, so that grape juice might be an alternative for Communion. For denominations that were very involved in the Temperance movement, grape juice became the standard at Communion.

Today many churches still use grape juice so there is no hesitation about recovering alcoholics and children participating in Communion. Some churches use only wine. Others provide both wine and grape juice, sometimes in different chalices, telling the congregation which is which. Churches that use both wine and grape juice in individual glasses may use red grape juice and white wine so that persons may distinguish between the two. With the development of sparkling juices, many churches find this a good compromise: it is still juice so all can partake; yet the sparkling bubbles give it a sense of celebration.

Allergies and Sensitive Immune Systems

Be aware that persons in your congregation may have allergies to wheat, eggs, or grape juice. It is not difficult to avoid foods to which persons are allergic or to substitute something similar. Be open and observant when persons consistently do not take one of the elements, and pay attention to discussion of children's allergies. Then, with pastoral care, quietly work to meet the need so that all persons feel welcome to the table to eat and drink.

What to Do with Leftover Elements

There are several possible ways to handle elements that are left over after all have received. The first is to use what was already blessed in the service as the elements to be used to "extend the table" to shut-ins, those hospitalized, and those who had to miss worship due to work schedules, sick children, or other reasons. This is an important ministry of the church and may be carried out by the pastor, deacon, or trained lay members.

Second is to offer the leftover bread to be reverently consumed by members of the congregation in the narthex after worship. Children can be taught what "reverently consumed" looks and acts like, and this can be a special time.

Third is to return the elements to the earth, following the Scripture in 2 Samuel 23:16, where water is poured on the ground as an act of worship. This is usually done by "watering" a plant or bush outside the church with any leftover juice or wine, and by breaking up the bread to feed the birds.

THE COMMUNION VESSELS

As told in the Acts of the Apostles, Communion was part of a larger fellowship meal in the early church, just as it was at the last supper Jesus had with his disciples. The vessels used would have been those used by a normal family for special meals, or as we might say today, the "good china." This meant in early times, cups made of glass and woven baskets. After Constantine became Christian in the fourth century, vessels for Communion gradually became more ornate—gold and silver, with precious stones sometimes imbedded in them. When the Reformation took hold in the 1500s, some groups returned to everyday household items, including wooden plates and cups, in an attempt to be more like the early church.

Today, all types of materials are used for Communion vessels. The use of special metals, such as gold and silver, remind us that this is a holy feast where we want to use our best to honor God. The use of ceramics, especially earthenware, reminds us that God is the creator of heaven and earth, and that the elements of bread and wine grow out of the earth. The use of glass enables the congregation to see the wine and gives a celebrative sparkle to the table.

The Paten

The plate that holds the bread for Communion is called the paten. It may be large enough to hold a single loaf of bread that will feed all present or smaller to hold wafers. When Communion is served around an altar rail, there may be a number of smaller patens to hold bits of bread or wafers within reach of several persons. It is also appropriate to have the bread in a basket, as may be seen in the many catacomb drawings of Communion in the early church.

Communion Linens

When the bread is put on the altar table before the service, a white linen cloth, about the size of a large dinner napkin, may cover it. This cloth is removed before beginning the Great Thanksgiving or Communion prayer. When serving by intinction (see below) there should be as many linen cloths available as there are servers, so that they may each hold the bread with a cloth.

In churches where Communion is celebrated infrequently, it is traditional to change the altar cloths to white. Now that many Protestant churches are celebrating Communion more frequently, it is common to keep the color of the season on the altar table and add a smaller white linen cloth over that color.

The Chalice and Related Vessels

The cup that holds the wine or grape juice for all present is called the chalice. Sometimes a pitcher is used to pour wine or juice into several chalices that will be used for serving by intinction; this pitcher may be called a flagon, ewer, or cruet. The main distinction between the three is their top: flagons have a lid, ewers are open pitchers, and cruets are generally smaller, with a stopper. Pouring from a pitcher reminds us of the pouring of water at our Baptism, a reminder that our sins are forgiven by the blood of Christ. The use of a single cup reminds us that we are all one body; multiple chalices enable intinction at several stations. In the second half of the 1800s, concern about germs and the spread of disease led to the patenting in 1894 of individual glasses for use during Communion. These are prepared before the service, ready to be served, and may be placed around an altar rail or in a serving tray.

A Caution about Disposable Vessels

There is a temptation today to use disposable individual glasses, plates, and paper napkins for Communion. This should be avoided for several reasons. This is a special holy meal, one that honors the God who made us and Jesus who died and was raised for us; it deserves better than throwaway vessels. Communion is also a means of honoring God who made us and all creation; adding *trash* from this meal does not do that.

Communion Kits for Pastors

There are small "Communion kits," sold in Christian bookstores, for pastors to use for visitation in homes or hospitals. They usually contain a small paten and individual glasses as well as a container for the wine or grape juice. Keep these clean and ready to use.

METHODS OF OFFERING COMMUNION

The early church manuscripts that give directions for Communion speak of people coming forward to receive Communion from servers in front of the altar table. Standing in the early church was most common, as there were not pews, and standing represented the freedom given to us in resurrection. Kneeling appears not to be a necessary part of Communion in the early years. It was introduced much later into worship in general, moving into the Middle Ages. During the Reformation, some reform-ers moved long tables and benches into churches for Communion so people might sit and commune. This led some churches to build a rail in front of or around the altar, which allowed persons to receive Communion near the altar while kneeling.

Intinction

Churches today practice a wide variety of ways of offering Communion, each of which has validity and historic precedence. Intinction follows the early church in inviting persons forward to receive the elements from servers; first receiving the bread, then dipping it in the chalice and eating it. It involves pairs of servers, stationed around the congregation for ease of movement. It is best if persons are free to get up and move to the servers as they are ready; ushers are not necessary. The practice of intinction lifts up several aspects of Communion: Communion is a gift that God gives to us and we respond to that gift by coming forward; we are served by each other as sharers in the body of Christ; we stand as resurrected persons and in solidarity with Christians around the world.

Using an Altar Rail

Receiving Communion at an altar rail gives the congregation a chance to come forward in response to God's gift of Communion and to kneel if so desired. It also creates a sense of community. At the altar rail, Communion can be served in two ways. First, servers can come around, placing the bread in the uplifted hands of per-sons and then bringing the cup for intinction. Often when this is done, persons leave after receiving and taking time to pray if desired; then others fill in the spaces left. Thus persons still may kneel, being humble before God, but there is the experience of being served, which emphasizes our reception of God's gift.

In a second method of receiving at an altar rail, the elements are placed prior to the service around the rail, generally with small patens of wafers and individual cups. Chunks of bread from

one loaf may also be spread around after the Fraction—or breaking of the bread after the Great Thanksgiving—for persons to
pull a piece off, with individual glasses already poured and ready.
This method is generally accompanied by table dismissals, a brief
prayer as each table finishes; then the next group comes forward.
Examples of table dismissals can be found throughout the following chapters. The nature of this method lends itself to the community aspect of Communion, gives opportunity for kneeling,
and fits with the words of Jesus to "Take, eat, this is my body."

Providing Time for Additional Prayer after Receiving

Whether persons receive by intinction or around an altar rail,
time and provision for kneeling for additional prayer can be an
important part of Communion. If the church has an altar rail, station the intinction servers so that persons can go to the rail after
receiving if so desired. If the tradition is to receive around the
altar rail, and if additional time for prayer near the altar table is
desired, consider shifting to the first method of serving around
the altar table, which gives individuals the freedom to leave
when they are ready after receiving. Other options for providing
worshipful time during the distribution of Communion are to
sing hymns that are familiar to the congregation, either by reference to hymnals in the bulletin, or to:
- use a verse or two of hymns known by heart;
- have the choir lead in an anthem with a refrain that the
  congregation can join;
- suggest that the congregation re-read the Scriptures for the
  day;
- suggest prayer concerns to be lifted up during this time; or
  simply call for silence for prayer and meditation.

Receiving in the Pews

In some congregations it is traditional to receive Communion
while sitting in the pews. This generally involves ushers who pass

patens of bread or wafers down the pews. Often persons will hold their bread or wafer until all have received a piece, then eat as one body as the pastor says, "This is the body of Christ. Take and eat." Then the ushers come back with trays of individual glasses that are passed down the rows. Generally the pastor says the words "This is the blood of Christ, the sign of the new covenant" as that begins so that persons can drink the wine or juice as soon as they receive it. This method of Communion symbolizes God coming to us in the presence of Christ. Eating the bread together symbolizes our oneness as the unified body of Christ; drinking the cup as we receive it acknowledges our individuality while still uniting us in Christ. These congregations may want to include times of silence before or after the distribution of the elements for prayer and meditation.

Serving One Another
and Receiving in a Circle

Communion can be particularly meaningful when persons gather around the table or the sanctuary, in a circle, for the prayer. This works well for retreats, small Bible or study groups, or congregations up to about forty persons. If done in the sanctuary, the beginning of the service could take place in the pews and then persons would gather around the Communion table or the sanctuary after the passing of the peace or following the offertory.

It is best if the congregational responses in the prayer are either known by heart or can be briefly taught or sung, so that hymnals, bulletins, or worship books don't need to be used. Examples of Great Thanksgivings appropriate for this kind of distribution may be found below.

During the distribution, each person breaks off the bread for the person on their right, gives it to them saying appropriate words, and passes the bread to the left. The chalice follows behind, with the person on the left holding the chalice for the person on their right, saying appropriate words to them, as the person on the right dips bread in the chalice. Then the chalice is also passed to the left. Although this may sound complicated, it can be easily learned, as the pattern is simply "serve right, pass left." The complexity comes in how the first persons handle the bread and chalice; it is probably best if the pastor or presider helps things to get started correctly and then receives Communion last. Because everyone will speak during this distribution, singing would be distracting during this time, especially in a small group.

SERVICES OF COMMUNION

Services of Communion may also be called Services of Word and Table, because they begin with hearing the Word of God as revealed in Scriptures and end with gathering around the Communion table. Most churches find that their services fall into the broad outlines of a fourfold pattern:

Gathering: often includes welcome, singing, call to worship, and prayers; may include announcements

Hearing the Word: through Scripture, singing, anthems, prayers, and sermon

Responding to the Word: through offering, prayer, singing, commitment, and Communion

Sending Forth: often includes closing hymn, benediction or blessing, and dismissal; may include announcements

Even in a brief service of Communion, elements of worship such as Scripture reading, meditation, prayer, and singing are appropriate and prepare us to come to God's table.

Some Common Questions about the Service of Holy Communion

How do we learn about worship and Communion when we sit in a congregation? Sometimes we attend Sunday school or other education classes where we can ask questions and get information. Sometimes pastors will preach about what is happening in the service so that we can better understand it biblically and theologically. Sometimes, if we are young or new to church, someone in the congregation might sit with us, and explain things as we go through the service. Sometimes our church newsletter or bulletin can provide a space for learning.

The following are questions that arose in congregations where the author has worshiped. For the last several years, she has written columns for the monthly church newsletter to answer some of these questions. You may reprint them in your church newsletter, use them in a confirmation or other education class, or reflect on them from the pulpit.

When does the Communion part of the service actually begin?

In some ways, Communion begins as we gather at the church or place where the service will be held. All the prayers, Scriptures, and songs are part of our "communion" with God and with one another.

Some scholars say the actual Communion begins with the "taking" of the elements of bread and cup, either receiving them from persons from the congregation or uncovering them, if they are already on the Communion table. Others would say that Communion begins with the invitation of persons to the table. This may immediately precede the Great Thanksgiving after the elements are received or may precede a time of confession and pardon, followed by passing of the peace.

Words of invitation may be:

- You that truly and earnestly repent of your sins, and are in love and charity with your neighbors, and intend to lead a new life, following the commandments of God, walking from this day forward in God's holy ways, draw near with faith to this table.
- Christ our Lord invites to his table all who love him, who earnestly repent of their sins, and who seek to live in peace with one another.
- This is the table of Christ. All who seek to be in fellowship with him and with each other are invited and welcome.

If your denomination or congregation has any restrictions on who may come to the table, say those words here or have them printed in the bulletin.

Why do some pastors and Communion servers wash their hands before Communion? Is this because of germs?

In the Jewish tradition that Jesus followed, men washed their hands before praying, to symbolize their coming before God with clean hearts and hands (see Psalm 24:4). Some churches follow this ancient tradition by providing a pitcher of water, someone to pour the water, a basin to catch the water, and towels so that the pastor's hands may be washed before saying the Great Thanksgiving.

It may be helpful to recapture this tradition that Jesus followed, and this reminder of our Baptism, in the pouring of the water. In addition, it may help some churches feel more comfortable sharing the elements of bread and common cup. Some churches also gather the intinction servers to have water poured over their hands, either with the pastor before the prayer, or after the Communion prayer and immediately before serving.

Because of the original linkage of Baptism and Communion, it is appropriate to use water when following this tradition. Using antiseptic liquids or disposable hand wipes loses this link to Baptism and to prayer. Washing hands at the Communion table is not primarily an avoidance of germs: studies of Communion by health professionals have shown no increase in the spread of germs when persons partake by intinction. The potential of spreading germs is also lessened when only one person's hands touch the bread to pull off pieces (rather than everyone pulling off their own). The only increase of germs happens when the pieces of bread are too small, so that in dipping into the cup, persons' fingers go into the wine or juice. This can be easily avoided by breaking off pieces of bread large enough so that doesn't have to happen. This practice has the added symbolic benefit of reminding us that God's grace is not stingy and small, but abundant.

Why do we have prayers of confession before having Communion?

Communion is a reminder of all that God has done for us, in saving us from sin and through acts of grace and mercy.

Confession reminds us of our place as human beings: we are not God, we fall short of God's hopes and intentions for us, we hurt others by our actions or our inactions, and we are in need of God's mercy for our own peace of mind.

Confession gives us an opportunity to be honest—with God, ourselves, and as the church—about our shortcomings, both personal and communal, so that we may know God's forgiveness and pardon in passing the peace of Christ and in partaking of Communion.

What's happening in Communion after we confess our sins?

Silence, which lets us each in our own way confess our individual failings. Then the pastor reminds us that we as a congregation are forgiven. We remind the pastor that he or she is forgiven too.

As people who have been pardoned, we leave our sins with God and don't pick them back up. We renew our commitment to try to live more Christlike lives. We pass peace to our neighbors in the pews, spreading the love and reconciliation of God's Spirit to all.

What's happening when we pass the peace in worship?

One of the oldest Christian traditions is passing the peace of Christ in worship by an embrace or holy kiss. Five of the letters to the early church include this reminder in their closing: Romans 16:16, 1 Corinthians 16:20, and 2 Corinthians 13:12 say, "Greet one another with a holy kiss." First Thessalonians 5:26 reads "Greet all the brothers and sisters with a holy kiss" while 1 Peter 5:14 says "Greet one another with a kiss of love." Some Communion services tell us to "offer each other signs of reconciliation and love." When we pass the peace during worship, it is the peace of Jesus Christ himself that we are modeling and demonstrating, to those we know, and to those who are strangers to us. This peace of Christ is that of people who know themselves to be forgiven and loved by God. "The peace of Christ be with you" and the response "And also with you" are traditional, but any words that greet another in the name of Christ and bring him alive in our midst are appropriate. Most often, persons shake hands or embrace, but even a smile or wave can pass Christ's peace around.

How are the elements presented within the service?

Sometimes the elements for Communion are prepared before the service and left on the altar table and around the Communion rail. When this occurs the elements are often covered with linen cloths.

Other congregations have the bread and wine or juice brought forward when the offering is brought forward. This involves persons in addition to the ushers: Communion stewards, the persons who baked the bread, or other laypersons. It symbolizes our offering of bread and wine or juice to God to use, just as God uses our monetary gifts. When this happens, the offering plates are either carried back out to an office or put on a small side table, so that only the gifts of bread and wine are on the altar table. The pastor and deacons or Communion servers accept the bread and wine or juice and put them on the table.

If your congregation has not previously brought the gifts in during the service, natural times to add this practice would be:

Epiphany: to echo the gifts brought by the Magi

Christmas, Palm Sunday, or Easter (when processions occurred in the early church): to echo the shepherds going to Bethlehem, Jesus' triumphal entry into Jerusalem, or the women going to the tomb and finding it empty

Thanksgiving: to echo the Jewish tradition of bringing the firstfruits of harvest to God

What is happening when the pastor breaks a loaf of bread or large wafer after the Communion prayer?

This action, called the Fraction, is the third of the four actions of Communion: taking, blessing, breaking, and giving. It reminds us of the brokenness of the world, of Christ being broken in the crucifixion, and of the need to break open our hearts to receive Christ. The action is sometimes accompanied by words from Scripture, but may be most effective when done in silence. There is no need here to lift the cup, as both the bread and cup have been blessed in the Great Thanksgiving.

What is the role of the ushers in Communion?

Ushers have different roles during Communion services, depending on how the elements are distributed. If Communion is distributed to persons seated in pews, ushers are responsible for passing the trays with the elements among the congregation and then taking some for themselves in order to partake. If the pews do not have receptacles for the empty glasses, the ushers return and pass the trays to collect the glasses.

When groups or tables receive Communion at an altar rail, ushers are often responsible for motioning persons to go forward and keeping track of how full each table is so that each person or row sent forward may find room. When Communion is received individually at an altar rail (usually when time for prayer is given), ushers are less necessary. Either way, ushers may need to be stationed by any steps to assist persons coming forward.

If Communion is served by intinction, the primary role of the ushers is to keep track of those persons who will need the elements to be brought to them because of mobility issues. Ushers may either alert the pastor or other servers, or they may be trained to bring the elements to those who need to remain in the pews. Sensitivity is required because sometimes a person may not come forward to the altar rail, not because of mobility issues, but because of a personal spiritual struggle or question. No one should feel forced to receive Communion.

Should the pastor take Communion first or last? What about servers, ushers, and the choir?

In some traditions, the pastors receive Communion first to demonstrate their own need of this sacrament or to prepare themselves to serve others; this was the tradition we inherited from the Middle Ages.

More recently, many pastors have chosen to model the role of Jesus at the table as the host, who serves the guests first and then partakes. This resonates with our understanding of servant leadership, relating to Jesus washing the feet of his disciples to demonstrate that he came to serve (John 13:3-17).

Servers, ushers, and the choir generally observe whichever pattern the pastor follows. All of these have *servant* and *leader* roles in this meal: the servers clearly, the ushers to help the people come forward or to serve those who remain in the pews, and the choir to assist in the service and by singing. One variation on this is if the choir is singing an anthem during the distribution (or leading the congregation in song), the distribution may flow more smoothly if they partake first and then continue singing as the table is reset after everyone has partaken.

What about children?

Various denominations and congregations have different practices about the presence of children during Communion. Those who baptize infants and children tend to include children in Communion; since they are baptized they are full members of the body of Christ and thus welcome at the table. Those who delay Baptism until an age of accountability or understanding tend to not include children in Communion until they have been baptized; some of these churches include a blessing on children instead of their participation in eating. In the early church, persons first took Communion immediately after they were baptized, so there is a historic understanding that Baptism precedes Communion. Many churches, however, practice what is known as an "open table," which means that the table belongs to Jesus and all who wish to follow him are welcome to come and commune.

Congregations need to talk about their denominational position and their own understandings. In one sense, no one ever fully understands Communion because it is so rich in meaning and practice; so to ask children to understand is to require something even adults cannot do. And many persons who have had experiences of being excluded from Communion will argue for opening the table.

Whatever invitation is offered needs to be clear, and all persons need to be taught the meanings of Communion and how to partake reverently. Children's sermons, Sunday school curricula, or even just the availability of picture books that explain Communion can be helpful to children and their parents.

How do we receive the bread at Communion?

Here are the Scripture accounts of giving of the bread at the Last Supper:

> While they were eating, Jesus took a loaf of bread, and after blessing it he broke it, gave it to the disciples, and said, "Take, eat; this is my body." (Matthew 26:26)

> While they were eating, [Jesus] took a loaf of bread, and after blessing it he broke it, gave it to them, and said, "Take; this is my body." (Mark 14:22)

> Then [Jesus] took a loaf of bread, and when he had given thanks, he broke it and gave it to them, saying, "This is my body, which is given for you." (Luke 22:19)

> And when [Jesus] had given thanks, he broke it and said, "This is my body that is for you. Do this in remembrance of me." (1 Corinthians 11:24)

John has no account of the Last Supper, but rather a long prayer by Jesus and him washing the disciples' feet. Echoes of Communion are heard in John 6:22-59, however, when Jesus says, "I am the bread of life."

The church has understood a number of things from these verses: Jesus is the host at the feast of Communion. It is Christ who feeds us and he becomes a part of us in the eating. The giving of the bread to the disciples has long been the tradition in Communion, where we are given bread (and the cup) rather than having to grab it for ourselves. These Scriptures also give Communion servers words to say:

- This is Christ's body that is for you.
- Take, this is Christ's body.
- Take, eat, this is Christ's body.
- This is Christ's body, given for you.
- This is the bread of life.

How do we receive Communion by intinction?

Intinction, the practice of dipping the bread into the cup, is one of the oldest methods of receiving Communion. It was revived in the modern day during World War II, in the field. We come forward to receive Communion in response to God's Word and offer of abundant life in Jesus Christ; this is one way we respond. We stand when receiving Communion in intinction because we are people of the Resurrection, children of God. If one of your family members or friends is serving, feel free to go to that station; it can be an extra blessing. As you wait in the line for Communion, pray for those you pass by and for those who wait in lines for food each day; whether at a soup kitchen or in war-torn countries—waiting for food from the UN, Red Cross, or UMCOR. If you would like to kneel at the altar for additional prayer after receiving the bread and juice, please feel free to do so. Otherwise return to your pew, thankful to God.

When you come forward to receive the bread, one tradition is to come with your hands together, palms up, with the fingers overlapping, making a cradle or throne for the bread, which represents Christ. The servers will give you a piece of bread big enough that you can dip into the cup without getting your fingers in the juice. (If it's big enough for two bites that's okay—God's love for you is abundant!)

Traditionally, it is appropriate to say "Amen" or "Thanks be to God" or even just "Thank you" in response to the servers who give you the bread and present the cup. Cup your free hand under the bread after dipping, so the juice doesn't drip.

How do we serve Communion by intinction?

Remember that this is an act of service and of ministry. Look persons in the eye as you offer them this gift of communion with God and with each other.

If you are serving the bread, pull off a large enough piece so that the person dipping the bread into the cup will not get their fingers in the juice. For children, reach down to their level, and say, "This reminds us of Jesus" or "This is God's love for you" or

"The bread of heaven." Other things to say when you are serving the bread (see also above):
- The body of Christ, the bread of heaven.
- *Name*, the body of Christ, given for you.
- *Name*, this is the bread of life.
- Jesus Christ, the bread of heaven.
- This is the body of Christ, the living bread.
- The body of Christ, the bread of life.
- This is the bread that unites us into the body of Christ.
- The body of Christ preserve your soul and body unto everlasting life.

Serving the cup: for children, lower the cup to their level, and say "This reminds us of Jesus" or "This is God's love for you" or "The cup of salvation." Other things to say when you are serving the cup:
- The blood of Christ, the cup of salvation.
- *Name*, the blood of Christ, given for you.
- *Name*, this is the cup of salvation.
- Jesus Christ, the cup of salvation.
- This is the blood of Christ, the saving cup.
- The blood of Christ, the cup of blessing.
- This is the cup of the new covenant, of new beginnings.
- The blood of Christ preserve your soul and body unto everlasting life.

When everyone has been served, check that there is no one in the congregation who needs to be served in their pew. Then give each other Communion, with the one serving saying the words over the bread and cup for the one who is partaking.

Traditional Parts of the Great Thanksgiving, also Known as the Communion Prayer or the Prayer of Consecration

In Dom Gregory Dix's massive 784-page book, *The Shape of the Liturgy*, he concludes that four actions have prevailed in

21

Communion liturgies throughout history: taking, blessing, break-ing, and giving. This prayer of blessing has been a defining one for the church: shaping persons in faith as they come to Communion, week after week in some denominations; telling and retelling the history of the Christian faith to the faithful and to new believers; invoking the presence of the Creator of the uni-verse and inviting that presence to come into the elements and our gathering as church; and sustaining the people of God for ministry in the world.

There are many models for the blessing or Great Thanksgiving throughout the history of the church, from very brief to rather lengthy. Some of the elements included in this prayer at different times in history are:

- Opening dialogue between presider and people, passed down from the early church, acknowledging the presence of God and inviting the congregation to give thanks and praise
- Thanksgiving to God the Father for the wonders of creation, redemption, and sanctification (drawing on Jewish traditions of blessing prayers)
- Congregational affirmation, made up of two parts, that God is holy. The first part is often called the *Sanctus* (from the Latin word for holy, recalling Isaiah 6). The second is often called the *Benedictus* (from the Latin word for blessing, recalling Jesus' entry into Jerusalem on Palm Sunday). An alternative or addition to the Sanctus and Benedictus is the *Gloria in Excelsis* or "Glory be to God on high," also known as the Larger Gloria, the Greater Gloria, or Canticle of God's Glory. The Gloria in Excelsis takes its text from Luke 2:14 and John 1:29.
- Thanksgiving for the redemptive work of Jesus Christ on earth
- The Words of Institution, according to New Testament tradition, usually in some version of 1 Corinthians 11:23-25, Matthew 26:26-30, Mark 14:22-25, or Luke 22:14-20
- Remembering the redemptive work of Jesus Christ in his life, ministry, passion, death, resurrection, and ascension;

also called the *Paschal Mystery* or *Anamnesis* (from the Greek word for remembrance that calls into being in the present)
- Congregational affirmation of the work of Jesus Christ, past, present, and future; often called the *Memorial Acclamation*, *Mystery of Faith*, or *Paschal Mystery*
- Recognition of the work of the Holy Spirit at Pentecost in bringing the church into being
- Invocation of the Holy Spirit on the community and on the elements of bread and wine, often called the *Epiclesis* (the Greek word for invocation)
- Recommitment of the church to the work of God
- Reference to the communion of saints
- Prayers for the whole church and the world
- Sometimes these prayers were followed by the congregation's plea for God's mercy, called the *Kyrie* (from the Greek word for Lord). These words may instead be incorporated into the time of confession and pardon during worship, before the Great Thanksgiving.
- A traditional congregational prayer asking Christ as the Lamb of God to forgive our sins and grant us peace, sometimes called the *Agnus Dei* (from the Latin for Lamb of God)
- Prayer for Christ's return and the manifestation of God's reign
- A Doxology or words of praise in the name of the Trinity
- Congregational affirmation by "Amen"

Opening Dialogue

The traditional words for the opening dialogue are:

The Lord be with you.
And also with you.
Lift up your hearts.
We lift them up to the Lord.
Let us give thanks to the Lord our God.
It is right to give our thanks and praise.

Alternative openings for the Great Thanksgiving include:
>The Lord is here. **God's Spirit is with us.** Let us pray.
>God is with you. **And also with you.** Let us pray.
>Almighty and merciful God, we thank you for your presence in our midst as we gather in praise and thanksgiving to you.

Sanctus and Benedictus
The traditional words for the first congregational affirmation, the Sanctus and Benedictus, are:
>Holy, holy, holy Lord, God of power and might.
>Heaven and earth are full of your glory.
>Hosanna in the highest!
>Blessed is the One who comes in the name of the Lord.
>Hosanna in the highest!

An alternative Sanctus, taken from Isaiah 6:3:
>Holy, holy, holy, is the LORD of hosts:
>the whole earth is full of God's glory.

Another alternative Sanctus, just a little longer, also without the Benedictus:
>Holy, holy, holy, Lord God of hosts:
>Heaven and earth are full of your glory!
>Glory be to you, O Lord most high!

Gloria in Excelsis
This canticle may replace the Sanctus and Benedictus or may be used earlier in the Communion service. It may be said or sung. The traditional words are from Luke 2:14 and John 1:29, and echo the Agnus Dei (Lamb of God):
>Glory be to God on high, and on earth peace, goodwill to all.
>We praise thee, we worship thee, we glorify thee,
>>we give thanks to thee for thy great glory:
>O Lord God, heavenly King, God the Father Almighty.

>O Lord, the only begotten Son, Jesus Christ;
>>O Lord God, Lamb of God, Son of the Father,
>>who takes away the sins of the world, have mercy upon us.

Thou who takes away the sins of the world, receive our
   prayer.
Thou who sits at the right hand of God the Father, have
   mercy upon us.

For thou only art holy; thou only art the Lord.
Thou only, O Christ, with the Holy Ghost,
   are most high in the glory of God the Father. Amen.

Words of Institution

Words of Institution tell the story of how Communion was
established and what it means for the followers of Jesus Christ.
Here are four options for the Words of Institution:

Matthew 26:26-28

> While they were eating, Jesus took a loaf of bread, and after
> blessing it he broke it, gave it to the disciples, and said, "Take,
> eat; this is my body." Then he took a cup, and after giving
> thanks he gave it to them, saying, "Drink from it, all of you; for
> this is my blood of the covenant, which is poured out for many
> for the forgiveness of sins."

Mark 14:22-24

> While they were eating, he took a loaf of bread, and after bless-
> ing it he broke it, gave it to them, and said, "Take; this is my
> body." Then he took a cup, and after giving thanks he gave it
> to them, and all of them drank from it. He said to them, "This
> is my blood of the covenant, which is poured out for many."

Luke 22:19-20

> Then he took a loaf of bread, and when he had given thanks,
> he broke it and gave it to them, saying, "This is my body,
> which is given for you. Do this in remembrance of me." And
> he did the same with the cup after supper, saying, "This cup
> that is poured out for you is the new covenant in my blood."

1 Corinthians 11:23b-26

> The Lord Jesus on the night when he was betrayed took a loaf
> of bread, and when he had given thanks, he broke it and said,
> "This is my body that is for you. Do this in remembrance of
> me." In the same way, he took the cup also, after supper, say-
> ing, "This cup is the new covenant in my blood. Do this, as

often as you drink it, in remembrance of me." For as often as you eat this bread and drink the cup, you proclaim the Lord's death until he comes.

Memorial Acclamation or Mystery of Faith

There are a number of Memorial Acclamations that are used in churches, to be said by the entire congregation. Here are some that are most common:

- Christ has died; Christ is risen; Christ will come again.
- When we eat this bread and drink this cup, we proclaim your death, Lord Jesus, until you come in glory. (Adaptation of 1 Corinthians 11:26)
- We remember Christ's death. We proclaim his resurrection. We await his coming in glory.
- Dying you destroyed our death; rising you restored our life. Lord Jesus, come in glory.
- Christ, by your cross and resurrection you have set us free. You are the Savior of the world.

Kyrie

Traditional words for the Kyrie may be said in English:

Lord, have mercy.
Christ, have mercy.
Lord, have mercy.

Or in Greek (pronounced as follows: Kyrie=kirēā; Christe=kristā; eleison=ə'lāəsən):

Kyrie eleison.
Christe eleison.
Kyrie eleison.

Agnus Dei

Because the intent of the Agnus Dei is included in the Gloria in Excelsis, ordinarily both would not be used in the same service. Traditional words for the Agnus Dei are:

Lamb of God, who takes away the sins of the world,
have mercy on us.

Lamb of God, who takes away the sins of the world,
    have mercy on us.
Lamb of God, who takes away the sins of the world,
    grant us your peace.

This may also be said or sung responsively, as follows:
Lamb of God, who takes away the sins of the world,
    have mercy on us.
Lamb of God, who takes away the sins of the world,
    have mercy on us.
Lamb of God, who takes away the sins of the world,
    grant us your peace.

An alternative version might be:
Jesus Christ, Lamb of God, have mercy on us.
Jesus Christ, bearer of our sins, have mercy on us.
Jesus Christ, redeemer of the world, give us your peace.

The Fraction

The Fraction is really meant to be an action, unaccompanied by words. However, some traditions are accustomed to words accompanying the action. When words are said during the Fraction, the following may be used:

- Because there is one loaf, we, who are many, are one body, for we all partake of the one loaf.
- The bread which we break is a sharing in the body of Christ.
- Christ broke open his life for us.

Welcome to the Table following the Great Thanksgiving

After the Fraction, the presider may welcome persons to the table with words such as:

- All things are ready. Come and feast!
- The holy things of God for the holy people of God. Come!
- Come to the joyful feast of the Lord.
- The gifts of God for the people of God.

- Christ our Passover is offered for us. Therefore let us keep the feast.
- Draw near to this table with faith.

Four Orders for Constructing the Communion Portion of a Worship Service

These orders are provided as guidelines in planning the Communion portion of your worship service. Each incorporates the four essential actions of taking, blessing, breaking, and giving. Within that framework, there are a number of options for several parts of the service, as may be seen below. It is possible to take the various parts of the service from this introduction and the prayers that follow in this book and develop a variety of services. The important thing is to approach your planning and the service reverently, in thanksgiving for this gift of our Creator to us, the life, death, and resurrection of Jesus Christ, that by the power of the Holy Spirit we might be in Communion with the Holy Trinity.

1. This is the order followed in many churches.
    Invitation to Communion
    Confession, Pardon, and Passing the Peace
       Optional: Kyrie
    Offering of Tithes, Offerings and the Elements of Bread
       and Cup
    The Great Thanksgiving
       Opening Dialogue or Sentence
       Thanksgiving to God the Father for salvation history
          Sanctus and Benedictus
       Thanksgiving for Jesus Christ, his person and works
          Words of Institution
          Anamnesis (Remembrance) and Memorial Acclamation
       Thanksgiving for the actions of the Holy Spirit
       Epiclesis (Invocation) of the Spirit on the Bread, Cup,
          and congregation
       Concluding Doxology
    The Lord's Prayer

The Fraction (Breaking the Bread)
Words of Welcome to the Table
Giving the Bread and Cup
    Optional: Agnus Dei (Lamb of God)
    Optional: Table Dismissals
Prayer after Receiving

2. This order provides for persons to use hymnals, bulletins, or overheads for the Great Thanksgiving responses and then to gather, after passing the peace, in a circle around the altar or sanctuary in order to receive.
    (Confession and Pardon earlier in the service, during the gathering section)
    Invitation to Communion
    Taking of the Elements of Bread and Cup
    The Great Thanksgiving
        Thanksgiving to God the Father for salvation history
        Sanctus and Benedictus
        Thanksgiving for Jesus Christ, his person and works
        Words of Institution
        Anamnesis (Remembrance) and Memorial Acclamation
    Epiclesis (Invocation) of the Spirit on the Bread, Cup, and congregation
    Concluding Doxology
    The Lord's Prayer
    Passing of the Peace
    The Fraction (Breaking the Bread)
    Words of Welcome to the Table
    Giving the Bread and Cup

3. This order provides the Words of Institution as a warrant for the service, first reminding the congregation why it is that we gather for this celebration.
    (Confession, Pardon, and Passing the Peace earlier in the service, during the gathering section)
    Taking of the Elements of Bread and Cup
    Invitation

Optional: Opening Dialogue
Anamnesis (Remembrance) and Words of Institution
The Great Thanksgiving
    Thanksgiving to God the Father for salvation history
        Sanctus and Benedictus
    Thanksgiving for Jesus Christ, his person and works
        Memorial Acclamation
    Epiclesis (Invocation) of the Spirit on the Bread, Cup, and
        congregation
    Concluding Doxology
The Lord's Prayer
The Fraction (Breaking of the Bread)
Giving the Bread and Cup

**4. This is the simplest order, suitable for less formal gatherings
or Communion with shut-ins or in hospitals.**
    Setting the Table and Taking the Elements of Bread and Cup
    The Great Thanksgiving and Blessing God for the gift of
    Communion
    The Fraction (Breaking the Bread) and Giving the Elements
    of Bread and Cup

CHAPTER TWO

COMMUNION SERVICES FOR HOLY DAYS AND SEASONS IN THE LITURGICAL/CHURCH YEAR

ADVENT

Advent is the season of four Sundays preceding Christmas. We anticipate the coming of the Christ, both the first time over 2000 years ago in Bethlehem and the Second Coming in the future.

Great Thanksgiving for First Sunday of Advent

This prayer is based on Psalm 80:1-7, 17-19 and Mark 13:24-37 and fits the lectionary for the First Sunday of Advent during Year B (2008, 2011, 2014, 2017, and 2020). The congregational response—Restore us, O God; let your face shine, that we may be saved—is from Psalm 80:3.

The Lord be with you.
And also with you.
Open your hearts.
We open them to the Lord.

31

Let us give thanks to the Lord our God.
It is right to give our thanks and praise.
It is right and a good thing to give thanks to you,
    Source of Light and Life.
We are the work of your hands; we are all your people.
Restore us, O God; let your face shine,
    that we may be saved.
You, O God, are faithful and have given us grace and light
    through Jesus Christ
But we turned away; we sinned before you.
Restore us, O God; let your face shine,
    that we may be saved.
Meet us, Holy One, in this meal
    that we may be restored to right relationship with you.
Join us together
    as the body of your beloved son, Jesus Christ.
Keep us wide-eyed for the day of your coming,
    that we may know your salvation.
Shine through us, Light of the World.
Send the flame of your Spirit on us and on these gifts of
    bread and cup.
Transform us into a people of hope, love,
    and justice for your world.
Restore us, O God; let your face shine,
    that we may be saved.
To you we pray, Source of Light and Life,
    through Jesus Christ, the Light of the World,
    In the light of your Holy Spirit,
    one God now and forever. **Amen.**

Great Thanksgiving for Second Sunday of Advent

This prayer is based on Isaiah 11:1-10, Psalm 72:1-7, 18-19, Romans 15:4-13, and Matthew 3:1-12 and fits the lectionary for the Second Sunday of Advent in Year A (2007, 2010, 2013, 2016, and

2019). The response—Blessed be the Holy One, (or Blessed be our God) who alone does wondrous things—comes from Psalm 72:18.

Faithful God,
> who gives hope and encouragement to your people
> through your prophets, Jesse and John:

Call us to repent, for your kingdom of heaven is near.

Blessed be the Holy One,
> **who alone does wondrous things.**

The spirit of wisdom and understanding rested
> on human flesh in Jesus Christ.

He is the true vine, rooted in your love, O God.

He gave us the fruit of his life and death,
> as he consecrated the cup of life for us.

Grow us as your branches, Holy One,
> that we may be rooted in Christ and grounded in you.

Blessed be the Holy One,
> **who alone does wondrous things.**

By the power of your Holy Spirit fill these gifts
> of bread and cup with joy and peace,
> that all the world may abound in the deep hope
> which you alone can give.

Blessed be the Holy One,
> **who alone does wondrous things.**

Blessed be God's glorious name forever.

Blessed be the Holy One,
> **who alone does wondrous things.**

May God's glory fill the whole earth,
> this church, and our lives. **Amen.**

Great Thanksgiving for Third Sunday of Advent

This prayer can also be used for other Sundays of the Advent season.

God is with you.

And also with you.

Lift up your hearts.

We lift them up to the Lord.
Let us give thanks to the Lord our God.
It is right to give our thanks and praise.
It is right to give you thanks and praise, Gracious God.
You created us and loved us, even when we turned away.
Through your prophets you promised to send us a savior.
Prepare our hearts and minds to receive your Incarnation,
    that we may know you through Jesus Christ and sing with
        all the saints in glory:
Holy, holy, holy Lord, God of power and might.
Heaven and earth are full of your glory.
Hosanna in the highest!
Blessed is the One who comes in the name of the Lord.
Hosanna in the highest!
Holy are you and blessed is your son, Jesus Christ.
He came and lived among us, teaching and healing,
    showing us new ways to live and love.
At his final meal with his disciples,
    Jesus took a loaf of bread,
    and when he had given thanks,
    he broke it and gave it to them, saying,
    "This is my body, which is given for you.
    Do this in remembrance of me."
Jesus did the same with the cup after supper, saying,
    "This cup that is poured out for you is
        the new covenant in my blood."
In remembrance and thanks for this gift of Jesus Christ,
    we give ourselves to you, O God,
    as we proclaim the mystery of faith:
Christ was promised; Christ is born;
        Christ will dwell among us.
Pour out your Holy Spirit on this bread and cup,
    and on us your children.
Form us into your body, the church,
    that we may be your body in the world.
Through Jesus Christ, with the Holy Spirit,
    all honor and glory is yours, Almighty God,
    now and forever. Amen.

Great Thanksgiving for Fourth Sunday of Advent

This prayer is based on Luke 1:26-38 and Luke 1:47-55 (the Magnificat) and fits the lectionary for the Fourth Sunday of Advent in Year C (2006, 2009, 2012, 2015, and 2018). The Words of Institution may be used during the Invitation to the Table or during the Fraction.

God is with you.
And also with you.
Open your hearts.
We open them to the Lord.
Let us give thanks to the Lord our God.
It is right to give our thanks and praise.
It is right and a joyful thing always and everywhere
       to give you thanks, gracious God.
You, Mighty One, have done great things for us,
    and holy is your name.
Your mercy is for those
    who honor you from generation to generation.
Throughout history
    you have helped your people
    in remembrance of your mercy,
    according to the promises you made to our ancestors.
Blessed be the Lord God of Israel,
    who has looked favorably on his people
    and redeemed them.
Mary, pregnant with the child Jesus, proclaimed God's glory:
God has shown strength with his arm,
    and scattered the proud in the thoughts of their hearts.
God has brought down the powerful from their thrones,
    and lifted up the lowly.
God has filled the hungry with good things
    and sent the rich away empty.
Blessed be the Lord God of Israel,
    who has looked favorably on his people
    and redeemed them.

Look favorably on us, Mighty One,
  and through your child Jesus Christ redeem us.
Fill us and this meal with your Holy Spirit,
  that we might dwell in your mercy
  and follow in your ways.
Through Jesus Christ,
  in the power of the Holy Spirit,
  all honor and glory is yours, Holy God,
  now and forever. **Amen.**

Resources for Advent

Congregational songs for singing during the services
  "Let All Mortal Flesh Keep Silence," translated by Gerard
  Moultrie
  "O the Depth of Love Divine" by Charles Wesley
  "Shine, Jesus, Shine" by Graham Kendrick

Spoken congregational responses
  • Restore us, O God; let your face shine, that we may be
  saved. (Psalm 80:3)
  • Blessed be our God, who alone does wondrous things.
  (Psalm 72:18)

Congregational songs for use as responses
  "Gloria in excelsis Deo" refrain from "Angels We Have
  Heard on High," traditional French carol
  "O come, let us adore him" refrain from "O Come, All Ye
  Faithful," traditional carol
  "Rejoice, rejoice, Emmanuel shall come to thee, O Israel"
  refrain from traditional carol, "O Come, O Come,
  Emmanuel"

*Memorial Acclamation for Advent through Transfiguration
(the Sunday before Ash Wednesday)*
  • Christ was promised, Christ is born,
  Christ will dwell among us.

Congregational songs for singing during the distribution
"Prepare the Way of the Lord" from Taizé
"Shine, Jesus, Shine" by Graham Kendrick
"This Little Light of Mine," traditional African American
  spiritual

Table dismissals
• Go from this place, to tell the world the good news of
  Christ who is coming.
• Tell the world: Emmanuel is coming to live among us!
• May Christ, the Sun of Righteousness, shine upon you.
• Go, and spread the good news of the coming
  of the reign of God.

CHRISTMAS

Christmas Eve and Day are the celebration of God coming in
human form in the person of Jesus, also known as the Incarnation.

Great Thanksgiving for Christmas Eve or Christmas Day, Option One

This prayer is based on Isaiah 9:2-7, Titus 2:11-14, and Luke 2:1-20.
God is with you.
And also with you.
Lift up your hearts.
We lift them up to the Lord.
Let us give thanks to the Lord our God.
It is right to give our thanks and praise.
On a night like tonight
  we have much to thank you for, Gifting God:
For you sent your Child to shine among us
  while we were still under the shadow of death.
You broke the yoke of sin and loneliness that burdened us.
You dwelt among us in justice and truth,
  giving grace and peace.

37

And so we join the angels' song to the shepherds:
Glory to God in the highest heaven
    and peace on earth to all of good will.
(or sing the refrain from "Angels we have heard on high")
Teach us, Child of Bethlehem, Prince of Peace,
    to follow your example of righteous living
        and good will to all.
As you broke your life open in our midst at Christmas,
    as Jesus grew to share bread with his disciples and followers,
    so we remember you as we break bread
        together this night.
Be among us as we proclaim the mystery of faith:
Christ was promised; Christ is born;
    Christ will dwell among us.
At this table unify our hearts and lives
    that we may be your people
        who return to the world glorifying and praising you
        through our living,
Wonderful Counselor, Mighty God, Everlasting Spirit,
Three-in-One. Amen.

Great Thanksgiving for Christmas Eve or Christmas Day, Option Two

This prayer is based on Isaiah 9:2-7, Titus 2:11-14, and John 1:1-14.
God is with you.
And also with you.
Lift up your hearts.
We lift them up to the Lord.
Let us give thanks to the Lord our God.
It is right to give our thanks and praise.
On a night like tonight
    we have much to thank you for, Gifting God:
For you sent your Child to shine among us
    while we were still under the shadow of death.
You broke the yoke of sin and loneliness that burdened us.

38

You dwelt among us in justice and truth,
   giving grace and peace.
And so we join the angels' song to the shepherds:
Glory to God in the highest heaven
   and peace on earth to all of good will.
(or sing the refrain from "Angels we have heard on high")
Help us to grow in the image of your Love, which made us.
We thank you for the mystery of Incarnation:
In the beginning was the Word.
The Word became flesh and dwelt among us.
We have seen your glory,
   the glory of grace and truth.
Fill this night with your Holy Spirit
   that we may know you in the breaking of bread
      and drinking of the cup
   and see you incarnate among your children gathered here.
Purify for yourself a people of your own who are eager
   to do good.
Make us to be those people, for we are yours.
Loving God, Incarnate Word, and Present Spirit,
   One God, now and forever. Amen.

Resources for Christmas Eve and Christmas Day

Congregational songs for use as responses
   "Come and worship" refrain from "Angels from the Realms of
   Glory"
   "Jesus your king is born" refrain from "'Twas in the Moon of
   Wintertime," traditional Huron carol by Jean de Brebeuf
   "Noel, noel" refrain from "The First Noel," traditional carol
   "O come, let us adore him" refrain from "O Come, All Ye
   Faithful," traditional Latin carol

Congregational songs for singing during the distribution
   Opening verses of any familiar carols
   "Glory to God (Gloria a Dios)," traditional Peruvian carol

Words for the Fraction and pouring of the cup
- At the Fraction, as presider lifts and breaks the bread:
  - In the breaking of the bread, God breaks into our world.
- As presider pours the drink:
  - In the pouring of the cup, the Spirit is poured out on the church.

Table dismissals
- Go, tell it on the mountain: Jesus Christ, the Savior of the world, is come!
- Arise and let Jesus Christ be born in you and in your living.
- Go and live as people who have seen the glory of the Lord.

NEW YEAR'S

Great Thanksgiving for New Year's Eve or New Year's Day

This prayer is based on Revelation 21:1-6a including the response: You, O God, make all things new.

The home of God is among mortals.
We are glad God is here.
Let us give God thanks and praise.
We are thankful for our lives, and praise God for blessings toward us.
We are grateful to you, O God,
    Creator of the new heaven and new earth,
    and of gifts yet to come, more than we can even imagine.
You, O God, make all things new.
You dwell among us and call us to be your people.
You dry the tears from our eyes.
You take away the power of death.
You bring us through mourning and crying and pain
    to be with you.
You, O God, make all things new.

In a surprising gesture, you came in human form
    to dwell among us.
Through Jesus Christ, you turned the world upside down—
    healing our diseases,
    teaching us new ways of thinking,
    living with us into new ways of community,
    overcoming sin and death to rise again in newness of life.
We remember his life, death and resurrection
    with thanksgiving.
You, O God, make all things new.
Come now, with your Holy Spirit, and make us anew.
Release us from our old burdens of hate and sorrow.
Free us from our doubts and fears.
Transform us into your people, full of love and joy,
    ready to do justice and dwell with you.
You, O God, make all things new.
By your Spirit, bless these elements
    and use them in your transformation of us,
    that Christ may indeed dwell in us
    and we in You, Great God, Three-in-One. **Amen.**

EPIPHANY

Epiphany, recalling the first manifestation of God to the Gentiles, as the Magi visit the Christ Child, is observed January 6, or the First Sunday of January.

Great Thanksgiving for Epiphany, Option One

This prayer is based on Matthew 2:1-12.
God is with you.
And also with you.
Lift up your hearts.
We lift them up to the Lord.
Let us give thanks to the Lord our God.

It is right to give our thanks and praise.
God of shining glory,
　　you poured your light upon us
　　that the whole world might come to you and live in joy.
Yet we choose the shadows,
　　hiding your Good News and hoarding it.
With the rising of Christ's star
　　you call us, like the Magi,
　　to seek you anew and worship you.
And so we join the company of heaven and earth singing:
Holy, holy, holy, Lord God of hosts:
Heaven and earth are full of your glory!
Glory be to you, O God most high!
Holy are you and blessed is your Child, Jesus Christ.
In Jesus you took on human form.
Today we celebrate the revealing of your Incarnation:
　　to visitors from afar, seeking a king;
　　to those beyond the community of Israel,
　　　　even to the whole world;
　　and to your church, down through the ages.
Throughout life on earth, Jesus continued
　　　　to reveal your presence.
The glory of your presence and its power
　　　　to transform our lives
　　was given form and substance in the meal
　　　　that Jesus gave us:
On the night in which he gave himself up for us,
　　Jesus took bread,
　　and after blessing it he broke it,
　　gave it to them, and said,
　　"Take; this is my body."
Then Jesus took a cup, and after giving thanks
　　he gave it to them, saying
　　"This is my blood of the covenant,
　　　　which is poured out for you."
For your love, which is revealed to us in Jesus Christ,
　　　　we give you thanks

and offer ourselves to you as we proclaim
>the mystery of faith:
Christ was promised; Christ is born;
>**Christ will dwell among us.**
Pour out your Holy Spirit on these gifts of bread and cup
>that they may reveal your presence to us.
Pour out your Holy Spirit on us gathered here
>that we may reveal your presence in the world.
Through Jesus Christ, in the power of the Holy Spirit,
>**all honor and glory is yours, Holy Trinity,**
>>**now and forever. Amen.**

Great Thanksgiving for Epiphany, Option Two

This prayer is based on Isaiah 60:1-6, Ephesians 3:1-12, and Matthew 2:1-12.
>God is with you.
>**And also with you.**
>Lift up your hearts.
>**We lift them up to the Lord.**
>Let us give thanks to the Lord.
>**It is right to give our thanks and praise.**
>It is right and a joyous thing
>>to lift our hearts and hands to you,
>>God of Light and Love,
>>>in thanksgiving for your gift of grace.
>Before we knew the unsearchable riches of your child Jesus,
>>we walked in shadows and cloud.
>But now as you reveal radiance to the world,
>>we join the hymn sung in glory without end:
>**Holy God, Grace Revealed,**
>>**heaven and earth are full of your glory.**
>**Blessed is the One who comes in your name.**
>**Hosanna in the highest!**
>Blessed are you, Creator God, and blessed is your child Jesus.

While wise ones brought him gold, incense and myrrh,
   he grew to reveal to us countless treasures,
   radiant with life and grace,
   revealing the Shining Mystery which is You.
Jesus broke bread and broke open your love for us.
He blessed the cup and you poured out mercy for the world.
Christ was promised; Christ is born;
   Christ will dwell among us.
Come, Spirit, dwell among us, your sons and daughters,
   gathered here together to feast at this table.
Use us to reveal your gifts of love and light for the world.
God of the ages, shining among us, we are yours! Amen!

Resources for Epiphany

Congregational songs for singing during the services
   "Deck Thyself, My Soul, with Gladness" by Johann Franck
   "I Want to Walk as a Child of the Light" by Kathleen
      Thomerson
   "Now the Silence" by Jaroslav J. Vajda

Congregational songs for singing during the distribution
   "Now the Silence" by Jaroslav J. Vajda
   "This Little Light of Mine," traditional African American
      spiritual

Words for the distribution
- Know in this bread, God's glory.
- Know in this cup, God's joy.

Table dismissals
- Rise, shine, for your light has come.
- Let the glory of the Lord shine through your life.
- Go, and spread the good news of the reign of God.
- Go forth in God's Spirit
  that God's glory may shine over all nations.
- To you, Emmanuel, Gift of Life, we give thanks and praise.

- Go forth from this table as a child of God's light,
  shining in this world.
- May Christ gladden your heart
  with the good news of the reign of God.

BAPTISM OF THE LORD

Baptism of the Lord is celebrated on the Sunday after the Epiphany, thus after January 6. It considers how Jesus identified with us in receiving baptism from John and God's affirmation. It also marks the beginning of the ministry of Jesus.

Great Thanksgiving for the Baptism of the Lord, Option One

This prayer is based on Isaiah 42:1-9, Psalm 29, and Matthew 3:13-17 and fits the lectionary for the Baptism of the Lord for Year A (2007, 2010, 2013, 2016, and 2019). The response—The Holy One will give us strength. God will bless us with peace—comes from Psalm 29:11. The left and right sides of the congregation could say the two sentences responsively.

You, Lord God,
    created the waters and the dry land.
Your Spirit gave breath to Earth's people.
You planted justice on the Earth
    and sent the Messiah as a light to all people.
The Holy One will give us strength.
God will bless us with peace.
We come to Baptism for repentance,
    to turn from evil and oppression.
Jesus of Nazareth came to be baptized to fulfill the Word,
    and you, O God, anointed him
        with your Holy Spirit and with power.
The Holy One will give us strength.
God will bless us with peace.

As the Spirit descended like a dove,
    you, who are God,
        claimed Jesus as your beloved son
            and anointed him with favor.
Come, Spirit, to this table,
    claim us as your children.
Come, as you have come, to the table of your people
    throughout history, as we have made thanksgiving
        to you.
The Holy One will give us strength.
God will bless us with peace.
Pour out your favor upon us and on these elements,
    that we and the whole world may know your son
    and come to your glory.
Planter of Justice, Beloved Son, Spirit of Peace, Holy One,
    we are yours. **Amen.**

Great Thanksgiving for the Baptism of the Lord, Option Two

This prayer is based on Genesis 1 and Mark 1:4-11 and fits the lectionary for the Baptism of the Lord for Year B (2008, 2011, 2014, 2017, and 2020).

The Lord be with you.
And also with you.
Lift up your hearts.
We lift them up to the Lord.
Let us give thanks to the Lord our God.
It is right to give our thanks and praise.
It is right and a good and joyous thing,
        always and everywhere
    to give you praise, Creator of Heaven and Earth.
You took the formless Earth,
        swept across it with your mighty Spirit,
    and said, "Let there be light!" And there was light.
You separated the heavens and earth,
        and brought forth trees and plants.

You set sun, moon, and stars in the heavens,
    and called forth fish, birds, and all living creatures.
You made us, creatures of your own image,
        to live in communion with you.
We long for relationship with you,
        but in our humanness, we turn away.
Yet you remain steadfast,
        calling us again and again to turn to you.
For your ever-present grace and for all your mercies toward us,
    we join your people on earth and all the company of heaven
        in proclaiming your praise:
Holy, holy, holy Lord, God of power and might.
Heaven and earth are full of your glory.
Hosanna in the highest!
Blessed is the One who comes in the name of the Lord.
Hosanna in the highest!
Holy are you and blessed is your son, Jesus Christ.
In this season we remember your gift of Baptism:
    how Jesus, though without sin,
    went to be baptized by John in the Jordan.
Just as Jesus was coming up out of the water,
    he saw the heavens torn apart
    and the Spirit descending like a dove on him.
And a voice came from Heaven,
    "You are my Son, the Beloved; with you I am well pleased."
We saw his glory.
And we understood Jesus as your anointed one,
        as he took bread and cup and said,
    "Take, eat; this is my body."
    "Drink from this cup, all of you;
    for this is my blood of the covenant,
    which is poured out for the forgiveness of sins."
In remembrance and in thanks for your beloved Son
        and all his actions on our behalf,
    we bring our whole selves to you,
    as we proclaim the mystery of faith:
Christ has died; Christ is risen; Christ will come again.

Send your Spirit upon these gifts and on us your children.
Claim us as your own, that we may go forth as your
      representatives in the world,
    until Christ comes again in final victory.
Through Jesus Christ, with the Holy Spirit,
    all honor and glory is yours, Almighty God,
    now and forever. **Amen.**

TRANSFIGURATION

Transfiguration Sunday is typically celebrated the Sunday
before Ash Wednesday. It marks an event in Jesus' ministry when
his glory was revealed, in part, to Peter, James, and John. The
Scriptures for this event from the life of Jesus are Matthew 17:1-
9, Mark 9:2-9, Luke 9:28-36, and 2 Peter 1:16-21.

Great Thanksgiving for Transfiguration Sunday

The Lord is with you.
And also with you.
Lift up your hearts.
We lift them up to God.
Let us give thanks to the Holy One.
It is right to give our thanks and praise.
It is right and a good and joyful thing
Always and everywhere to give thanks to you, O God.
You created Heaven and Earth
    and made us to be your people.
Your glory settled on Mt. Sinai
    when you gave Moses the laws for your people:
glory, shining like a blazing fire
    for all the people below to see.
Like them, with your people on earth
    and all the company of heaven,
    we praise your name and join the unending hymn:

Holy, holy, holy, Lord God of hosts:
Heaven and earth are full of your glory!
Glory be to you, O Lord most high!
Holy are you and blessed is your son Jesus Christ.
In the midst of teaching and healing, Jesus took a day apart
    and went up onto a high mountain
        with Peter, James, and John.
Your glory settled on Jesus,
        making him to shine like the sun,
    telling the disciples that this Jesus was your son,
        the Beloved.
We seek to listen to him
    and we remember him now in the meal he gave us,
    as we proclaim the mystery of faith:
Dying you destroyed our death; rising you restored
    our life. Lord Jesus, come in glory!
Pour out your Holy Spirit on us gathered here
    and on these gifts.
Make them be for us a lamp shining in a dark place,
    until the day dawns and the morning star rises
        in our hearts.
By your Spirit make us one with Christ, one with each other,
    and one in ministry to all the world.
Blessing and honor and glory and power be yours,
    Holy God, now and forever. Amen.

ASH WEDNESDAY AND LENT

Ash Wednesday marks the beginning of the Lenten season. On this day we recognize our mortality and come before God with repentance. Historically, Lent is a season of 40 days (not counting Sundays) where the church focuses on what it means to commit ourselves to Jesus Christ through baptism and discipleship.

Great Thanksgiving for Ash Wednesday

The Lord is with you.
And also with you.
Lift up your hearts.
We lift them up to God.
Let us give thanks to the Holy One.
It is right to give our thanks and praise.
It is right and a good and joyful thing
    always and everywhere to give thanks to you, O God.
You created us to live in communion with you,
        yet we turned away.
You spoke through your prophet Joel:
    Return to me with all your heart,
    for I am gracious and merciful,
    slow to anger
    and abounding in steadfast love.
We come on this Ash Wednesday,
    knowing our failings
    but trusting in your steadfast mercies.
Thanks be to you, Holy God, for steadfast mercy.
You are holy and blessed is your child Jesus Christ.
Your Spirit flowed through his life as he became the bridge
        for our reconciliation.
In this season we remember his life and work.
We remember your gift of Baptism.
We reflect on the mystery of the cross,
We dare to ponder resurrection.
On his final evening with his disciples,
    Jesus took a loaf of bread,
    and when he had given thanks,
    he broke it and gave it to them, saying,
    "This is my body, which is given for you;
    do this in remembrance of me."
After supper Jesus did the same with the cup, saying,
    "This cup that is poured out for you is the new covenant
    in my blood."

In remembrance of these your mighty acts on our behalf,
we bring our whole selves to you,
as we proclaim the mystery of faith:
Christ has died; Christ is risen; Christ will come again.
Pour out your Holy Spirit on us
and on these gifts of bread and cup.
May this meal be for us
signs of your gracious mercy:
forgiveness of our sins and promise of salvation.
To you be all praise and glory, Holy God, now and forever.
Amen.

Great Thanksgiving for First Sunday in Lent

This prayer is based on Genesis 9:8-17, Psalm 25:1-10, 1 Peter 3:18-22, and Mark 1:9-15 and fits the lectionary for Year B (2008, 2011, 2014, 2017, and 2020). The response—Lead us in your truth and teach us, for you are the God of our salvation—is from Psalm 25:5. Possible sung responses include "Lead Me, Lord" by Samuel S. Wesley and the refrain of "Thy Word Is a Lamp unto My Feet" by Amy Grant and Michael W. Smith.

God of the Covenant,
you saved those on the ark through the flood
and gave them your sign of Covenant, the rainbow.
Through repentance and baptismal waters
we too have been saved,
and made signs of your New Covenant in Jesus Christ.
Lead us in your truth and teach us,
for you are the God of our salvation.
After Jesus was baptized in the Jordan,
your Spirit drove him out into the wilderness.
Like Jesus, we too are tempted.
Yet he showed us how to resist evil.
Lead us in your truth and teach us,
for you are the God of our salvation.
Coming out of the wilderness,
Jesus began proclaiming your good news, saying,

"The time is fulfilled,
   and the kingdom of God has come near;
   repent, and believe in the good news."
Lead us in your truth and teach us,
   for you are the God of our salvation.
Bring your reign near to us in this meal, Mighty Spirit.
Draw us together in the ark of your church,
   that we may be signs of your covenant in the world,
Covenanting God, Resisting Christ, and Saving Spirit,
   One God in Three. **Amen.**

Resources for Ash Wednesday and Lent

Congregational songs for singing during the services
   "Bread of the World in Mercy Broken" by Reginald Heber
   "Here, O My Lord, I See Thee Face to Face" by Horatius
   Bonar

Table dismissals
   • Arise and go, to live a sober and godly life.
   • Arise and go, knowing that Jesus Christ is walking with
   you.
   • May God grant you grace to grow in holiness.
   • May the crucified Christ give you the assurance that you
   are forgiven and loved.

PALM/PASSION SUNDAY

Palm/Passion Sunday has a twofold focus: to celebrate Jesus'
triumphal entry into Jerusalem (Matthew 21:1-11) and to anticipate his Passion: the work of Holy Week, the Last Supper, temptation, betrayal, arrest, trial, crucifixion, and death.

Great Thanksgiving for Palm/Passion Sunday

God of the Covenant,
   you created us and called us to be your people.

You raised up David as a leader of your people.
Lead us in your truth and teach us,
    for you are the God of our salvation.
This is the day on which the people of Jerusalem
    spread their cloaks on the ground,
    cut palm branches, and cried out:
"Hosanna to the son of David!
    Blessed is the one who comes in the name of the Lord!
    Hosanna in the highest!"
Like them, we praise you, O Christ,
    and acknowledge you to be our ruler.
Lead us in your truth and teach us,
    for you are the God of our salvation.
Bring your reign near to us in this meal, Mighty Spirit.
Draw us together in the praise of Jesus Christ
    who gave his life for our salvation
Through Jesus you made with us, Holy God,
    a new covenant by water and the Spirit,
    marked by his body, represented by this bread,
    and by his blood, represented by this cup.
Claim us
    that we may be signs of your covenant in the world,
Covenanting God, Blessed Christ, and Mighty Spirit,
    One God in Three. **Amen.**

HOLY (OR MAUNDY) THURSDAY

Some churches have a tradition of celebrating Communion on Holy Thursday (also called Maundy Thursday) around long tables, in remembrance of Jesus' Last Supper. The service may take place in the sanctuary if there is sufficient room or may take place in the fellowship hall. There are echoes in the Great Thanksgiving below of the Passover liturgy that may have been part of Jesus' experience. The elements might be either passed along the tables (with trays or by intinction) or persons may

come to stations to receive by intinction. It would be appropriate
to include a place and time for persons to kneel in prayer after
receiving if desired.

Great Thanksgiving for Holy Thursday

*This prayer is based on Exodus 12:1-4, 1 Corinthians 11:23-26, and
John 13:1-17.*

On this night, we gather
        as the Hebrew people gathered in exile
    to share the Lamb and celebrate your passing over them
        in mercy.
On this night, we gather amazed and humbled
    to have the dust of our souls washed by the servant Messiah.
We pause in our hurried lives to ask:
What wondrous love is this, O my soul,
    that caused Christ to lay aside his life for my soul?
We pass on tonight to children and strangers
    what we have received from you, Lord Jesus:
Who on the night you left us took bread
    blessed it, broke it
    and gave it to the disciples, saying,
    "Do this in remembrance of me,"
Who took the cup and said,
    "This is my life for you,
    share in its newness and remember me."
And so we remember:
    how you came to us, poor and vulnerable,
    how you taught us by story and example,
    how you fed us on hillside and seashore.
As we remember you,
    pour out yourself again to us
    and by your Holy Spirit make us living remembrances
        of your great love and life.
Fill us with a new understanding of love
    among all your children
    that others may see our witness and draw close to you.

Merciful Deliverer, Humble Servant,
and Love Among Us, Holy Trinity,
we give you praise and thanks. Amen.

Resources for Communion
on Holy Thursday

Congregational songs for singing during the service
"Deck Thyself, My Soul, with Gladness" by Johann Franck
"I Want to Walk as a Child of the Light" by Kathleen Thomerson
"Now the Silence" by Jaroslav J. Vajda

Congregational songs for singing during the distribution
"Now the Silence" by Jaroslav J. Vajda
"This Little Light of Mine," traditional African American spiritual

EASTER

Easter is the celebration of the resurrection of Jesus from the dead.

Great Thanksgiving for Easter Sunday

This prayer is based on Acts 10:34-43, Colossians 3:1-4, and Matthew 28:1-10. An alternative to the spoken "Alleluia" response would be to sing a familiar "Alleluia" (for example, the one by Jerry Sinclair) or one from Taizé.

Christ is risen!
Christ is risen indeed!
Lift up your hearts.
We lift them up to the Lord.
Let us give thanks to the Lord our God.
It is right to give our thanks and praise.

It is right and a joyful thing to praise you, Holy God,
   who through your Spirit anointed Jesus of Nazareth
   to tell your good news of grace and love
   through his life, death, and resurrection.
Alleluia!
Break open the tombs of our lives
      by your earthquake and lightning
   that we may know your power
   and take courage from Christ's resurrection
   to live new lives.
Alleluia!
Grant us the fear and hope of the Marys
      as they heard the angel's word:
Christ was not in the tomb!
Christ is risen!
Christ will go before us into the world!
Pour out your Spirit of resurrection on us
      and on these elements,
   that we may experience newness in our own lives
   and bear your good news to the world.
Alleluia!
Thanks be to you, God of creative newness!
Thanks be to you, Christ, reborn among us!
Thanks be to you, Comforting and Challenging Spirit!
Thanks be to you, Holy God, Three-in-One.
Alleluia! Amen!

Resources for Easter through the Great Fifty Days to Pentecost

   The time between Easter and Pentecost is called the Great
Fifty Days, a time of celebration of the meaning of resurrection
for our lives.

Congregational songs for singing during services
   "Become to Us the Living Bread" by Miriam Drury
   "Christian People, Raise Your Song" by Colin P. Thompson
   "O Thou Who This Mysterious Bread" by Charles Wesley

Congregational songs for use as responses
"Alleluia" by Jerry Sinclair
"Alleluia" by Fintan O'Carroll and Christopher Walker
"Alleluia," one of several from the Taizé Community or by Jacque Berthier
"Alleluia, Alleluia! Give Thanks to the Risen Lord" by Donald Fishel (refrain only)
"Christ the Lord Is Risen Today" by Charles Wesley (with the "Alleluias")
"Halle, Halle, Halle" from the Caribbean
"Alleluias" from "The Strife Is O'er, the Battle Done," music by Palestrina

Congregational songs for singing during the distribution
Any of the "Alleluias" listed above or others familiar to the congregation

Table dismissals
• Go and tell the good news: Christ has risen! Death has lost its power.
• To God belongs the victory. Alleluia!
• Arise and go, as those who have seen the Lord.

PENTECOST

Pentecost ends the Great Fifty Days of Easter and celebrates the coming of the Holy Spirit on the disciples and those gathered in Jerusalem after the Ascension of Jesus Christ. Most important, Pentecost is celebrated as the beginning of the church in the world.

Great Thanksgiving for Pentecost, Option One

God's Spirit is with you.
And also with you.
Lift up your hearts.

We lift them up to God.
Let us give thanks and praise to God.
It is right to give our thanks and praise.
It is right, and we are glad to be able to give you thanks,
      gracious God.
In the beginning,
   your Spirit moved across the waters,
   and creation began.
You made human beings in your image
   to live in community with you.
When we sinned and fell away,
   your Spirit called us back.
You promised always to be with us
   and sent your Spirit to fulfill that promise.
And so with people from all times and places,
   in every language,
   with all creation,
   we praise your name:
Holy, Holy, Holy God,
   Wind and Flame and Dove.
Heaven and earth are full of your glory.
Hosanna in the highest.
Blessed is the One who comes in the name of our God.
Hosanna in the highest.
Blessed is your child Jesus Christ
   in unity with you and the Holy Spirit.
At the baptism of Jesus in the Jordan,
   your Spirit descended on him like a dove,
   saying "This is my Beloved."
Jesus promised that when he left the disciples
   the Advocate, the Spirit of truth, would come.
It was this Spirit who descended with tongues of fire,
   like the rush of a violent wind
   on those gathered in Jerusalem
   on the day of Pentecost.
This was the beginning of your church,
   as Peter preached to the crowd
   and three thousand persons were baptized.

Through the church you have given us this meal,
    that we might remember Jesus
    who took bread, blessed it,
    broke it, and gave it to his followers saying,
    "This is my body, given for you."
Through the power of your Holy Spirit,
    generations have passed on this tradition
    that we might remember Jesus who said,
    "This cup is the new covenant in my blood."
It is your Spirit which enlivens the mystery of faith:
Christ has died; Christ is risen; Christ will come again.
Send your blessed Spirit on us gathered here
        and on these elements,
    filling us and them with your presence.
Enflame our hearts that we might be as the early church,
    ready to preach your good news to all the world,
    eager to live as your Spirit-filled people.
All praise and thanks,
    glory and honor is yours,
Holy Trinity, now and forever. **Amen.**

Great Thanksgiving for Pentecost, Option Two

Congregational Response: "Come, Holy Spirit, come!" or sing the refrain of "Spirit of God" by Steve Garnaas-Holmes.
    Great God of heaven and earth,
        Spirit which existed before time began,
    we give you thanks for all the blessings you have given us:
        the world we live in,
        the church,
        our families and friends,
        food and shelter,
        work and play.
Come, Holy Spirit, come!
Come now and be among us,
    just as Jesus Christ came and dwelt among us.

We remember how Jesus taught and healed,
  gathered disciples and ate with sinners.
Jesus promised us that he would send us an Advocate,
  the Spirit of truth,
    that we might know God's love for us.
Come, Holy Spirit, come!
After Jesus was resurrected from the dead,
  when he was at table
    with the disciples from the road to Emmaus,
Jesus took bread, blessed and broke it, and gave it to them.
Their eyes were opened, and they recognized him;
  and he vanished from their sight.
That same hour the disciples returned to Jerusalem
  and told what had happened on the road,
  and how Jesus had been made known to them
    in the breaking of the bread.
Come, Holy Spirit, come!
Fill this bread and cup with your presence, Holy Spirit,
  that we may know the presence of Christ
  and the love of God as we partake of this meal.
Come, Holy Spirit, come!
Fill us and this church with your energy and power,
  that we might spread the good news
    of God's forgiving love to all the world.
Come, Holy Spirit, come!
And with the Father and the Son,
  we will give you all the praise and glory forever. **Amen.**

Resources for Pentecost

Congregational songs for use during the distribution
  "We Are the Church" by Richard K. Avery and Donald S.
  Marsh
  "Spirit of the Living God" by Daniel Iverson
  "Veni Sancte Spiritus (Holy Spirit, Come to Us)" by Jacques
  Berthier of Taizé

Table dismissals
- Go, and translate the love of God
  for those who have not yet heard the good news.
- Go, in the power of the Holy Spirit
  to spread the good news of God's love.
- Go, and may the fire of the Holy Spirit
  burn brightly in your life.
- Go, and spread the good news of the reign of God
  to all the world.
- May the Spirit of truth lead you into all truth.

TRINITY SUNDAY

Trinity Sunday is celebrated on the Sunday after Pentecost, to give the church opportunity to concentrate on the mystery that is God, One-in-Three and Three-in-One.

Great Thanksgiving for Trinity Sunday, Option One

This prayer is based on Genesis 1, 2 Corinthians 13:11-13, and Matthew 28:16-20 and fits the lectionary for Year A (2007, 2010, 2013, 2016, and 2019).

Christ is risen!
Christ is risen indeed.
Lift up your hearts.
We lift them up to the Lord.
Let us give thanks to the Lord our God.
It is right to give our thanks and praise.
It is right and a good and joyous thing,
      always and everywhere
   to give you praise, Creator of heaven and earth.
You took the formless chaos,
      swept across it with your mighty Spirit,
   and said, "Let there be light!"

And there was light.
You separated the heavens and earth,
 and brought forth trees and plants.
You set sun, moon, and stars in the heavens,
 and called forth fish, birds, and all living creatures.
You made us, creatures of your own image,
 to live in communion with you.
We long for relationship with you, yet we turn away.
Still you remain steadfast, calling us again and again
 to turn to you.
For your prevenient grace and for all your mercies toward us,
 we join your people on earth
  and all the company of heaven
 in proclaiming your praise:
Holy, holy, holy Lord, God of power and might.
Heaven and earth are full of your glory.
Hosanna in the highest!
Blessed is the One who comes in the name of the Lord.
Hosanna in the highest!
Holy are you and blessed is your son, Jesus Christ.
You gave Jesus all authority in heaven and on earth,
 and so we follow him.
Jesus called us to make disciples of all nations,
 baptizing them in your Triune name,
 and teaching them to obey everything
  that you commanded.
Jesus promised to be with us always, to the end of the age.
On the day of his resurrection,
 he walked with two disciples to Emmaus
 and sitting at table with them,
  Jesus took bread, blessed it and broke it,
 and they saw the mystery of faith:
Christ has died; Christ is risen; Christ will come again.
Send your Spirit upon these, the gifts of your creation:
 grain, grapes, and us your children.
Strengthen us to do your will, to baptize and to teach,
 and to always walk with Jesus Christ.

Through him, with the Holy Spirit,
   all honor and glory is yours, Almighty God,
   now and forever. **Amen.**

Great Thanksgiving for Trinity Sunday, Option Two

This prayer is based on John 3:1-17 and fits the lectionary for Year B (2008, 2011, 2014, 2017, and 2020).

Christ is risen!
Christ is risen indeed.
Lift up your hearts.
We lift them up to the Lord.
Let us give thanks to the Lord our God.
It is right to give our thanks and praise.
It is right and a good and joyous thing,
      always and everywhere
   to give you praise, Creator of heaven and earth.
You took the formless chaos,
   swept across it with your Word and mighty Spirit,
   and said, "Let there be light!"
And there was light.
You separated the heavens and earth,
   and brought forth trees and plants.
You set sun, moon, and stars in the heavens,
   and called forth fish, birds, and all living creatures.
You made us, creatures of your own image,
   to live in communion with you.
We long for relationship with you, yet we fall into sin.
Still you remain steadfast,
   calling us again and again to turn to you.
For your inviting grace and for all your mercies toward us,
   we join your people on earth
      and all the company of heaven
   in proclaiming your praise:
Holy, holy, holy Lord, God of power and might.
Heaven and earth are full of your glory.

Hosanna in the highest!
Blessed is the One who comes in the name of the Lord.
Hosanna in the highest!
Holy are you and blessed is your son, Jesus Christ.
You loved the world so much,
>   that you sent Jesus to the earth,
>   so that everyone who believes in him
>   should not perish
>   but have everlasting life.
On the day of his resurrection,
>   he walked with two disciples to Emmaus
>   and sitting at table with them,
>   Jesus took bread, blessed it and broke it,
>   and they saw the mystery of faith,
>   which we now proclaim:
Christ has died; Christ is risen; Christ will come again.
Send your Spirit of truth upon these,
>   the gifts of your creation:
>   grain, grapes, and us your children.
Renew in us the second birth,
>   the birth of your Holy Spirit
>   that we may see your kingdom
>   and walk in your ways, Holy God.
Through Jesus Christ, with the Holy Spirit,
>   all honor and glory is yours, Almighty God,
>   now and forever. **Amen.**

Resources for Trinity Sunday

Table dismissals
- Rise to live in peace;
  and the God of love and peace will be with you.
  (2 Corinthians 13:11)
- Arise, and may the grace of Jesus Christ, the love of God, and the communion of the Holy Spirit, One God, be with you. (2 Corinthians 13:13)
- Arise and go in the name of Father, Son and Holy Spirit, the Triune God.

- Go from this place to proclaim the grace of Jesus Christ, the love of God who made us, and the power of the Holy Spirit, One God, now and forever.

WORLD COMMUNION SUNDAY

World Communion Sunday falls on the first Sunday of October, as churches around the world celebrate their oneness in Christ by gathering at the Communion table. For this service, it is appropriate to have persons bring breads from their countries of origin or countries where the church supports mission. Taking Communion with a different kind of bread may represent solidarity with another culture or remind us that church around the world is all one body of Christ. See the special Prayer of Confession in the Resources section that follows the Great Thanksgivings for World Communion Sunday.

Include a note in the bulletin or take the children's sermon time to explain the various breads and their origins. Some options to consider: rye bread, scones, cornbread, pita bread, tortillas, rice cakes, foccaccia, injera (from Ethiopia). Day-old bread can remind us of those in our own country for whom fresh bread is a luxury.

Display the breads on the altar table as the service begins. For the Fraction, choose bread that will break easily. Either prepare patens beforehand, with individual pieces (not too small) for dipping of each of the various kinds on each paten, or have servers help to do that after the prayer as people are preparing to come to the table. Do note that some of these breads will crumble easily.

Great Thanksgiving for World Communion Sunday, Option One

This prayer is based on Ephesians 4:4-6.
    The Lord be with you.
    And also with you.

Lift up your hearts.
We lift them up to the Lord.
Let us give thanks to the Lord our God.
It is right to give our thanks and praise.
God of all nations,
　　you created every person in your image
　　and called us by your Holy Spirit
　　to become one in Christ Jesus,
　　through Baptism and through faith.
In Jesus Christ, you showed us the way to live
　　with unique gifts and particularities,
　　yet in harmony with you and with each other.
You, O God, are indeed above all and through all and in all.
So, today we join with voices throughout the earth
　　　　and in heaven, saying:
Holy, holy, holy Lord, God of power and might.
Heaven and earth are full of your glory.
Hosanna in the highest!
Blessed is the One who comes in the name of the Lord.
Hosanna in the highest!
Holy are you and blessed is your child, Jesus Christ.
Jesus lived among us to show us your love:
　　caring enough to feed hungry persons,
　　stopping to touch persons in need of healing,
　　reaching out to those not like himself:
　　　　a Samaritan woman at a well,
　　　　lepers from another country,
　　　　those tortured by demons,
　　　　a father pleading for his daughter,
　　　　a woman from Syro-Phoenicia,
　　　　Zacchaeus, a tax collector,
　　　　a rich young ruler, and humble fishermen.
When people gathered to hear his teachings,
　　Jesus took bread, blessed it and broke it,
　　and gave it to them to eat, so that they might be fed.
When Jesus ate with his disciples for his final meal on earth,
　　they remembered his blessing on the multitude,

66

and listened as he told them:
"Take, eat, this is my body given for you."
They watched as Jesus took the cup, blessed it and said,
    "Take, drink, this is my blood of the new covenant,
    poured out for you and for the whole world
    for the forgiveness of sins."
After his death and resurrection,
    by the power of the Holy Spirit,
    the disciples told others through this meal,
    that Jesus was the Messiah, sent by God, for all humankind.
Remembering now, we proclaim the mystery of faith:
Christ, by your cross and resurrection
    you have set us free.
You are the Savior of the world.
Pour out your Holy Spirit on the table
    spread this day around this globe,
    and here spread with breads from around the world.
May all who partake, wherever they live,
    know the reconciling love of Jesus Christ.
May your church go forth from Communion with you
    to be one in Christ and one in witness to the world.
In your Holy Name we pray. Amen.

Great Thanksgiving for World Communion Sunday, Option Two

The congregational response may be sung using: "Amen, We Praise Your Name, O God (Amen Siakudumisa)" from South Africa; "Halle, Halle, Halle" from the Caribbean; or an "Alleluia" familiar to the congregation.

Almighty and merciful God,
    we thank you for your presence in our midst
    as we gather in praise and thanksgiving to you.
(Congregational Response)
Creator God, you made humankind in your image,
    with varied hues of skin, hair, and eyes,
    of varied heights and widths,
    with differing talents and gifts.

67

Yet all of us are beautiful in your sight.
We give you thanks for calling us to be your children.
(Congregational Response)
We thank you for sending Jesus Christ to live among us.
In his time on earth, Jesus reached out to all persons,
    poor and rich,
    children, women and men,
    sick and marginalized.
He taught us to do the same.
And he gave us this meal to remember him:
    taking a loaf of bread, giving thanks,
    he broke it and said,
    "This is my body that is for you.
    Do this in remembrance of me."
In the same way, he took the cup after supper, saying,
    "This cup is the new covenant in my blood.
    Do this, as often as you drink it, in remembrance of me."
We give you thanks for Jesus Christ and for this meal.
(Congregational Response)
We ask your Holy Spirit to come to the table
        spread around the world today:
Bless each person and bless our partaking
    that we may grow into your body,
    united in your love,
    to bring your reconciling peace to the whole world.
For these hopes and for all your promises given and kept,
    we give you thanks, Holy Trinity, now and forever.
(Congregational Response)

Resources for World Communion Sunday

Congregational songs for singing during the service

"Deck Thyself, My Soul, with Gladness," words by Johann
    Franck
"I Want to Walk as a Child of the Light" by Kathleen
    Thomerson
"Now the Silence," words by Jaroslav J. Vajda

Suggested congregational songs for singing during the distribution

"Now the Silence," words by Jaroslav J. Vajda

"This Little Light of Mine," traditional African American spiritual

Prayer of Confession for World Communion Sunday

All: God of mercy,
   we confess that we have not loved you
      with all our being.
We have done things which we ought not to have done,
   and we have left undone things which we ought
      to have done.
We have built walls between neighbors
      and between countries,
   and we have ignored the cries of those in need.
Forgive us and set us free,
   that we may live into the hope of your calling,
   that your reign may come on earth as it is in heaven.
Through Jesus Christ we pray. Amen.
One: Thanks be to God: Jesus died for our sins.
      We are forgiven!
All: We are forgiven. Thanks be to God.

Table dismissals

- Go to be God's peace in the world.
- Go to share God's love
  with all of God's children everywhere.
- Be at one with your brothers and sisters
  throughout creation.
- Go in the power of the Holy Spirit
  to shine God's love abroad.
- Go forth to meet the world that God loves.
- Go forth to be the presence of God in the world.
- Go into the world,
  rejoicing in the power of the Holy Spirit.

ALL SAINTS DAY

All Saints Day occurs on November 1 or the first Sunday of November. It is a time to consider all those who give us examples of Christian living. Many churches celebrate it as a time to remember persons in the faith who have died in the previous year.

Great Thanksgiving for All Saints Day

The congregational response—Blessing and glory and wisdom, thanksgiving and honor, power and might be to our God forever and ever!—is taken from Revelation 7:12.

You, O God created us and have brought your people
    through many trials:
Abraham and Sarah, Miriam and Moses,
Deborah and Isaiah, Peter and Mary,
Francis of Assisi and Clare,
Martin Luther and John Wesley.
Martin Luther King Jr. and Mother Teresa—
all attest to your providence and mercy
    and show us ways to live.
Blessing and glory and wisdom, thanksgiving and honor,
power and might be to our God forever and ever!
You came in human form to walk among us,
    teaching us the way to live as your children.
In Jesus Christ you showed us what holy living looks like,
    and gave us the sacraments of Baptism and Communion
    to remember and experience anew your presence,
    encouraging us to live in relationship to you.
Blessing and glory and wisdom, thanksgiving and honor,
power and might be to our God forever and ever!
In this meal we give you praise and thanks, Creator God,
    as we remember all those who have passed on into glory.
Pour out your Spirit,
    that this bread may be for us the bread of heaven,
and this cup,
    the cup of your new covenant in Jesus Christ.

Bind us together by your Spirit as your holy people,
    washed by your Baptism
and strengthened for holy living by this meal.
Blessing and glory and wisdom, thanksgiving and honor,
    power and might be to our God forever and ever! Amen.

Resources for All Saints Day

Congregational songs for singing during the service
    "Blest Be the Tie that Binds" by John Fawcett
    "For the Bread Which You Have Broken" by Louis F. Benson
    "In Christ There Is No East or West" by John Oxenham, to
    tune of African American spiritual
    "Let All Mortal Flesh Keep Silence," translated by Gerard
    Moultrie
    "This Is the Feast of Victory" by John W. Arthur

Congregational songs for use during the distribution
    "This Is the Feast of Victory" by John W. Arthur
    "You Satisfy the Hungry Heart" by Omer Westendorf and
    Robert E. Kreutz

Table dismissals
    • May God grant you grace to follow the saints
      in faith, hope and love.
    • Go to live as God's saints in the world today,
      by the grace of the Holy Spirit.
    • You are called to live as God's people in the world.
      Go strengthened by the great cloud of witnesses.

THANKSGIVING OR GENERAL USE

Great Thanksgiving for Thanksgiving Service or General Use

In the following prayer there is a list of some of God's many gifts to us.

Eight persons might be designated to share those words, noted in italics, or the presider may say them.

The peace of God, which surpasses all understanding, is yours.
Thanks be to God!
Let us give God praise and glory.
We praise God for the surpassing gift of Jesus Christ.
We thank you, God, for this meal that your child, Jesus,
gave us.
In it are represented your many gifts to us:
Gifts of daily food, part of your generous creation,
Commemoration of the time you gave manna in the
wilderness,
Remembrance of the times that Jesus fed the multitudes,
Recalling the sadness of the last meal he had with the
disciples,
A foretaste of the heavenly banquet that you have
promised,
Memories of mealtimes with friends
and with those who have gone before us,
Celebration of loving relationships,
a meeting place for us with you,
The promise that you will sustain us through all of life.
The gift of being able to come to your table
Prompts us to not forget those who are without food
and those who are not yet welcomed at your table,
Strengthens us for tasks of daily living,
Empowers us with your Spirit for the difficult times.
We want to know you, God.
We want to experience you, Jesus Christ.
We want to breathe you in, Holy Spirit.
Come, meet us now at this table,
pouring out your Spirit on us and on this bread and cup.
You alone have created us.
You alone nourish us.
You alone can guide us to be your children.
What we have is nothing, if you are not in our lives.
We give ourselves to you here and now.

Thank you for your great love given through Jesus Christ and given in this Communion. **Amen.**

Resources for Thanksgiving or General Use

Table dismissals
- Go and let your life be a blessing to all the world.
- Go and bless, as you have been blessed.
- Arise and live a life of gratitude.
- Give thanks with your life to your Creator.

GENERAL OR ORDINARY TIME

The following resources are appropriate for the General or Ordinary Time of the Christian year, after Epiphany until Lent and after Pentecost until Advent. This part of the Christian or liturgical year takes its name from the ordinal numbers (1st, 2nd, 3rd) formerly used to denote their position after Epiphany or Pentecost. Worship leaders should take care that Ordinary Time does not become static—the liturgical color for this season is green, reflecting the growth in which Christians are always involved.

Resources for General or Ordinary Time

Congregational songs for use as sung responses
"For the Beauty of the Earth," traditional or Communion refrain, by Folliot S. Pierpoint:
> Lord of all, to thee we raise
> this our hymn of grateful praise.
> —or—
> Christ our God, to thee we raise
> this our sacrifice of praise.

"Gloria" refrain from "Angels We Have Heard on High," traditional French carol
"He Is Lord," traditional
"Holy God of Cloud and Flame" refrain, by Ruth Duck and Carlton R. Young

"Majesty, Worship His Majesty" by Jack Hayford

"One Bread, One Body" refrain, by John B. Foley

"Take Our Bread" refrain, by Joe Wise

"This Is the Feast of Victory" refrain, translated by John W. Arthur

"To God be the glory" refrain ("Praise the Lord"), by Fanny Crosby

"You Satisfy the Hungry Heart" refrain, by Omer Westendorf

Congregational songs for singing during the distribution

"Come and Fill Our Hearts (Confitemini Domino)" by Jacques Berthier of Taizé

"Eat This Bread" by Jacques Berthier of Taizé

"Fill My Cup, Lord" by Richard Blanchard

"Holy God of Cloud and Flame" by Ruth Duck and Carlton R. Young

"In the Lord I'll Be Ever Thankful" by Jacques Berthier of Taizé

Any of the suggested congregational songs that might be used for sung responses

Words for the welcome to the table after the Great Thanksgiving

- Come, all things are ready!
- Come to the joyful feast of the Lord
- Holy things for God's holy people. Come!
- The gifts of God for the people of God.
- Christ our Passover is offered for us.
  Therefore let us keep the feast.
- Draw near to this table with faith.
- Jesus said, "I am the bread of life. Whoever comes to me will never be hungry, and whoever believes in me will never be thirsty." (From John 6:35)
- In Jesus Christ we have redemption through his blood, the forgiveness of our trespasses, and the richness of God's grace, lavished on us. Come, these gifts are for you! (From Ephesians 1:7)

Table dismissals

- May the body and blood of our Lord Jesus Christ give you strength and keep you in his grace and peace.
- Arise in thanksgiving to God for this holy mystery.
- You have been given God's own self in this meal. Go in peace.
- Go to live your life as one who belongs to Jesus Christ.
- The grace of the Lord Jesus Christ, the love of God, and the Communion of the Holy Spirit go with you.
- Rise to go and serve the Lord.
- Rise as freed persons to love and serve the Lord.
- Go out in the power of the Holy Spirit to serve the Lord.
- Go from this table in the power of the risen Christ.
- Go forth in the name of God.
- Go in peace to love and serve the Lord.
- Go from this table, empowered to do Christ's work in the world, to the glory of God.
- Go forth in hope, knowing that God goes with you.
- May the God of peace fill you with all joy and hope in believing.
- Christ is the vine and you are the branches. Go to abide and grow in him.
- Go forth in the peace that passes all understanding, the peace of Christ

CHAPTER THREE

COMMUNION PRAYERS FOR SPECIFIC EVENTS IN THE LIFE OF CHURCHES AND INDIVIDUALS

CONFIRMATION

As youth move toward confirmation, their first public profession of their Baptism, include training to be Communion servers in confirmation classes. On the day of confirmation, as you move into the Communion service with intinction, let the confirmands serve Communion in pairs. Give the congregation freedom to go to the station they choose, so that parents and siblings might receive Communion from their confirmand family member.

Great Thanksgiving for Confirmation Sunday, Option One

The Lord is with you.
And also with you.
Lift up your hearts.
We lift them up to the Lord.
Let us give thanks to the Lord our God.

It is right to give our thanks and praise.
It is right and a good and joyful thing, always and everywhere
    to give you thanks, Almighty God.
You claim us as your people,
        bathe us in forgiveness through Baptism,
    and draw us together into your church.
You call us to be your royal priesthood, a holy people,
    and you give us this holy meal as food for our journey.
Today these confirmands profess their faith
    and your presence in their journey.
Today they claim your gracious love for themselves
    and seek to live into a deeper and mature faith.
Give them your grace and peace,
    as they and we join with your people on earth
    and all the company of heaven to praise your name:
Holy, holy, holy Lord, God of power and might.
Heaven and earth are full of your glory.
Hosanna in the highest!
Blessed is the One who comes in the name of the Lord.
Hosanna in the highest!
Holy are you and blessed is Jesus Christ,
        who came to live among us.
As a young person, Jesus traveled with his family
        to Jerusalem,
    then stayed behind in the temple,
    sitting among the teachers, listening to them,
        and asking questions.
Jesus grew in wisdom and in years,
        and in divine and human favor,
    setting us an example of spiritual growth.
He calls us now to walk in God's ways on a journey of faith.
On the night before his own journey in the flesh ended,
    Jesus took a loaf of bread,
    and when he had given thanks,
        he broke it and said to his disciples,
    "This is my body that is for you.
    Do this in remembrance of me."

In the same way Jesus took the cup after supper, saying,
  "This cup is the new covenant in my blood.
  Do this, as often as you drink it, in remembrance of me."
In remembrance of Jesus Christ's gracious acts on our behalf,
  we offer ourselves to you, O God,
    as we proclaim the promises of faith:
Christ has died; Christ is risen; Christ will come again.
Pour out your Holy Spirit on all gathered here
  and on these gifts of bread and cup.
Make them be for us the body and blood of Christ Jesus,
    that we may be for the world the body of Christ,
      redeemed and reconciling.
Through Jesus Christ, with the Holy Spirit,
  all honor and glory is yours, Holy God,
    now and forever. Amen.

Great Thanksgiving for Confirmation Sunday, Option Two

We gather around this table today, Almighty God,
  to give you thanks.
You claim us as your people,
  bathe us in forgiveness through Baptism,
  and draw us together into your church.
You call us to be your royal priesthood, a holy people,
  and you give us this holy meal as food for our journey.
Today these confirmands profess their faith
  and your presence in their journey.
Today they claim your gracious love for themselves
  and seek to live into a deeper and mature faith.
Give them your grace and peace.
Now we join together to remember and experience anew
  the presence of the risen Christ in our midst at this table.
We give thanks for the gracious life of Jesus:
  teaching and healing, challenging and loving,
    dying and rising.

As we eat this bread and drink of this cup,
    pour out your Holy Spirit on us,
    that we may go forth to live as those claimed by you,
    your holy people, spreading holiness and wholeness
        in your world this day.
To God be the glory now and forever! **Amen.**

Resources for Confirmation

Congregational songs for singing during the distribution
"I Come with Joy" by Brian Wren
"In the Singing" by Shirley Erena Murray and Carlton R. Young
"Life-giving Bread" by Rick Manalo
"Take Our Bread" by Joe Wise
"Water, River, Spirit, Grace" by Thomas H. Troeger and O. I. Cricket Harrison
"We Are the Church" by Richard Avery and Donald Marsh

Table dismissals
- Go forth to live as those claimed by God.
- You have been called to be a royal priesthood.
- Live as God's holy people in the world.
- Go forth as forgiven and beloved people, that God may be known in the world.

COMMITMENT OR COMMISSIONING

Many congregations have opportunities throughout the year for personal or congregation recommitment. Some also commission various persons: Sunday school teachers, church leaders, those going on mission trips or projects, and leaders of men's, women's, and youth organizations. These are all appropriate times to include Communion and remind us of our ministry as part of the body of Christ.

Great Thanksgiving for Services of Commitment or Commissioning

This prayer is based on Matthew 28:16-20.

The Lord is with you.
And also with you.
Lift up your hearts.
We lift them up to the Lord,
   to give God thanks and praise.
It is right and a good and joyful thing
  always and everywhere to give you thanks,
   marvelous Creator.
You made us and came in Jesus
  to show us the way to live.
When we doubted,
  you reminded us of your constant presence.
Therefore, in celebration of your unending presence,
  we join your followers of all times and places:
Holy, holy, holy, Lord God of hosts:
Heaven and earth are full of your glory!
Glory be to you, O Lord most high!
Blessed is Jesus Christ,
  who demonstrated authority
  as he taught and healed
  and as he appeared to the disciples after his resurrection.
Christ still bids us to go to all people,
  to baptize and to teach,
  to walk in the way of God.
We remember Christ's authority among us,
  revealed in taking bread and cup
  to make them holy for us.
In joy, we proclaim your presence, God in Christ:
Dying you destroyed our death; rising
   you restored our life. Lord Jesus, come in glory.
Come now, Spirit of God,
  and fill this time and place with your presence.

Fill these elements and fill us,
  strengthening us
  to go where you send us
  and to bear your love to all the world.
**We give you thanks and praise, God of the ages,
  who graces us with your presence always. Amen.**

Resources for Services of Commitment or Commissioning

Congregational songs for singing during the service
  "Here I Am Lord" by Dan Schutte
  "Are Ye Able" by Earl Marlatt
  "Forth in Thy Name" by Charles Wesley
  "Go Forth for God" by John R. Peacey
  "God of Grace and God of Glory" by Harry Emerson Fosdick
  "Lord, Whose Love Through Humble Service" by Albert F. Bayly
  "Lord, You Have Come to the Lakeshore (Tú Has Venido a la Orilla)" by Cesareo Gabaraín
  "When We Are Living (Pues Si Vivimos)," traditional Spanish hymn
  "You Are the Seed (Sois la Semilla)" by Cesareo Gabaraín

Congregational songs for singing during the distribution
  "I, the Lord of sea and sky" verse from "Here I Am, Lord" by Dan Schutte
  "Lord, You Have Come to the Lakeshore (Tú Has Venido a la Orilla)" by Cesareo Gabaraín
  "Spirit of the Living God" by Daniel Iverson
  "When We Are Living (Pues Si Vivimos)," traditional Spanish hymn

Table dismissals
  • Go to serve God and your neighbor in all that you do.
  • Go, recommitted to doing the will of God.
  • Arise, knowing that God goes with you.
  • Arise in the power of the Holy Spirit to walk in God's ways.

RETREAT OR CAMP SETTING

Great Thanksgiving for Retreat or Camp Setting

This prayer uses the African American spiritual, "Kum Ba Yah (Come By Here)." Confession, pardon, and passing the peace are incorporated into this prayer, so they do not need to be done separately beforehand.

Sing: Kum ba yah, my Lord.
Come by here, Holy God, come by here.
We have gathered out of love for you,
    and out of need for you.
Sing: Someone needs you, Lord.
We know these particular needs, O God,
    in this community and in the world, and we name them
        now before you:
    *(Give time for persons to name the needs of the world, of the
        community, and of individuals.)*
Sing: Someone's crying, Lord.
We have sorrow, Lord Jesus,
    sometimes because that is part of human life,
    sometimes because we have messed things up.
You know our sorrows,
    because you lived a human life,
    you were betrayed by a disciple,
    arrested unfairly,
    beaten and crucified.
You showed us how to walk through trials with dignity
    and you gave us the promise that death and sin
        were not the end.
Sing: Someone's praying, Lord.
Forgive us our sins, O God.
By the power of your Holy Spirit,
    remind us again that we are baptized and washed clean.

By that same power, strengthen us to live new lives,
   lives that walk close to you.
Sing: You forgive us, Lord.
We give thanks for your powerful forgiveness
   that frees us to live unburdened.
Empower us to tell your good news to the world
      in word and in deed.
As forgiven and reconciled people,
   let us begin to spread God's good news
   by passing the peace of Christ.
Sing: We will pass your peace.
(Options: sing until passing of peace is completed or sing and then
      pass the peace)
Sing: Let us praise the Lord.
We give thanks for this meal,
   reminding us of the life of Jesus given for us.
As we come to feast with you,
   fill our need for you,
   strengthen our hope for living,
   and embrace us in your love.
Bind us together as your people, eager to do your will.
And we will give you all the praise and glory
      now and forever.
Sing: Let us praise the Lord.
(As the bread is broken, the presider may speak the Words of
   Institution):
While they were eating, Jesus took a loaf of bread, and after
blessing it he broke it, gave it to them, and said, "Take; this
is my body." Then he took a cup, and after giving thanks he
gave it to them, and all of them drank from it. Jesus said to
them, "This is my blood of the covenant, which is poured
out for you."

Resources for Retreat or Camp Setting

Congregational songs for singing during the service
   "Eat This Bread" by Jacques Berthier of Taizé
   "Fill My Cup, Lord" by Richard Blanchard

"He Is Lord," traditional
"In the Lord I'll Be Ever Thankful" by Jacques Berthier of
    Taizé
"Majesty, Worship His Majesty" by Jack Hayford
"One Bread, One Body" by John B. Foley
"Take Our Bread" by Joe Wise

IN HOSPITALS, HOSPICE, WITH SHUT-INS, AT TIMES OF CRISIS

It can be meaningful to include other familiar reminders of worship at these times: saying the Lord's Prayer together, singing a verse of "Amazing Grace" by John Newton, reading Psalm 23 or another favorite biblical passage. Depending on the tradition of those present and their ability to respond, space may be left for "Amen" by the participants at the end of any section of the following prayers.

Great Thanksgiving for Communion in a Hospital

God the Great Physician, we come into your presence
    to know your healing touch,
        the wholeness you alone can bring.
You made us and you know our bodies inside out.
You call us to be in relationship with you.
Forgive us for the times we have turned away.
Come to us now as we turn toward you.
We remember how Jesus showed compassion for the sick:
    how he made the blind to see,
    how he healed the daughters of Jairus
        and the Syrophoenician woman,
    how he healed ten lepers,
    how he healed a woman who touched
        the hem of his cloak,

how he told a lame man to take up his cot and walk,
how he raised Lazarus out of death,
how he shared food with his disciples in life-giving ways,
    giving them this meal to remember him.
And so, we remember your deep love for us,
    in the midst of illness and in this Communion.
Pour out your loving Spirit on us and on this bread and cup.
Make us whole persons, in relationship with you.
And like those Jesus healed,
        we will sing your praises now and forever. **Amen.**

Great Thanksgiving for Shut-ins, Those in Hospitals or Hospice

This prayer is based on Psalm 23.
    The Lord be with you.
    And also with you.
    God, you are our Good Shepherd,
        and with you we lack nothing.
    You make us to lie down in green pastures.
    You lead us beside still waters.
    You restore our souls.
    You lead us in the paths of righteousness
        for your name's sake.
    Even when we walk through the darkest valley,
        we fear no evil,
        for you are with us.
    We give you thanks for all these blessings
        and for all your promises toward us.
    You have prepared this table before us,
        set by Jesus Christ.
    Here we gather to feast with him,
        to remember his life given for us,
        his death atoning for us,
        and his resurrection freeing us.
    Come with your Holy Spirit to us and to this meal.
    Anoint us with your blessings that our cup may overflow.

Guide us from this time forward
in your ways, Good Shepherd.
Then, surely, goodness and mercy shall follow us
all the days of our lives,
and we shall dwell in your house,
gracious God, forever. **Amen.**

Great Thanksgiving for Communion in Times of Crisis

Response: Come, Lord Jesus!
God, who holds us all in the palm of your hand:
The circumstances of life are wrenching us away from you.
Call us back! Remind us that you walk with us
and that with you all things are possible.
Come, Lord Jesus!
We remember your Son Jesus standing trial,
being rejected and killed.
In Christ you felt our pain, O God.
Come, Lord Jesus!
Knowing he faced possible death,
Jesus left his followers this reminder of himself
and of your love,
as he said "This is my body given for you.
This is my blood shed for you."
Come, Lord Jesus!
Send your Spirit on these elements
that they may be for us Christ's presence,
broken but whole,
in pain yet in hope.
Come, Lord Jesus! Amen.

EARTH DAY

The celebration of Earth Day each spring gives Christians an opportunity to consider God's good creation and our stewardship of it.

Great Thanksgiving for Earth Day

This prayer, based on Genesis 1, would be appropriate for other times focused on creation as well, such as outdoor services and camp settings.

Christ is risen!
Christ is risen indeed!
Lift up your hearts.
We lift them up to the Lord.
Let us give thanks to the Lord our God.
It is right to give our thanks and praise.
It is right and a good and joyous thing,
  always and everywhere
  to give you praise, Creator of heaven and earth.
You took the formless chaos,
  swept across it with your mighty Spirit,
  and said, "Let there be light!" And there was light.
You separated the heavens and earth,
  and brought forth trees and plants.
You set sun, moon, and stars in the heavens,
  and called forth fish, birds, and all living creatures.
You made us, creatures of your own image,
  to live in communion with you.
We long for relationship with you,
  but in our humanness, we turn away.
Yet you remain steadfast,
  calling us again and again to turn to you.
For your grace and for all your mercies toward us,
  we join your people on earth
  and all the company of heaven
  in proclaiming your praise:
Holy, holy, holy Lord, God of power and might.
Heaven and earth are full of your glory.
Hosanna in the highest!
Blessed is the One who comes in the name of the Lord.
Hosanna in the highest!
Holy are you and blessed is your son, Jesus Christ.

Your Spirit flowed through his life
   as he became the bridge for our reconciliation.
In this time we remember his life and work.
We remember your gift of Baptism.
We reflect on the mystery of the cross.
We dare to ponder resurrection.
Especially we recall how Jesus took grain,
   grown by your sunshine and rain,
   ground by human hands into flour,
   mixed with water and made into bread,
   in honor of him who is the Bread of Life.
We recall how Jesus took the cup,
   with grapes grown in your sunlight,
   trod into juice for drinking,
   that we might know you and never thirst again.
And taking bread and cup,
   blessing and breaking them,
   Jesus gave them new meaning
   as he said:
"Take, eat; this is my body."
"Drink from this cup, all of you;
   for this is my blood of the covenant,
   which is poured out for the forgiveness of sins."
In remembrance of all your mighty acts on our behalf,
   we bring our whole selves to you,
   as we proclaim the mystery of faith:
Christ has died; Christ is risen; Christ will come again.
Pour out your Spirit on these, the gifts of your creation:
   grain, grapes, and us your children.
Make us see your touch in all of creation
   and let us bring your light into every darkened shadow.
Through Jesus Christ, with the Holy Spirit,
   all honor and glory is yours, Almighty God,
   now and forever. **Amen.**

CHILDREN AND YOUTH

Great Thanksgiving for the Beginning of the School Year

This prayer is based on Luke 2:41-52 and Proverbs 8–9.

God is with you.
And also with you.
Lift up your hearts.
We lift them up to the Holy One.
Let us give thanks to God who is All Wise.
It is right to give our thanks and praise.
It is right always and everywhere to give you thanks,
    Holy One.
From your vast wisdom you created the universe,
    the complexity of stars and oceans,
    the wonder that is humankind.
You showed your people the ways of wisdom,
    how to live in peace and joy.
When we turned away and counted on our own wisdom,
    which was unwise,
    you waited to welcome us back in your love.
As we begin this new school year,
    bless all those who seek to learn:
    children, youth, adults, and teachers.
Bless those who prepare the learning environment:
    teachers, principals, counselors, secretaries,
    tutors, cooks, custodians,
    nurses, bus drivers, and crossing guards.
Bless those who support students:
    parents, grandparents, and this church community.
Help us all to grow in your wisdom and in your ways.
Remind us as we come to this table,
    that Christ is in the bread we eat and in the cup we drink,
    here now, and each day, wherever we are.

By your Spirit of Wisdom, keep us open
to your Word and ways.
In the name of Jesus Christ we pray. Amen.

Resources for the Beginning of the School Year

Congregational songs for singing during the service
"Holy Spirit, Truth Divine" by Samuel Longfellow
"How Firm a Foundation," anonymous
"Immortal, Invisible, God Only Wise" by Walter Chalmers Smith
"This Is a Day of New Beginnings" by Brian Wren and Carlton R. Young
"Thy Word Is a Lamp Unto My Feet" by Amy Grant and Michael W. Smith
"Praise the Source of Faith and Learning" by Thomas H. Troeger

Table dismissals
• Go in the knowledge and love of Jesus Christ,
  who is the wisdom of God.
• Arise to grow in wisdom and in years,
  and in favor with God.
• Go in the knowledge of God to live wisely.
• Go from this table to live in wisdom and charity
  with your neighbors.

Great Thanksgiving for Children's Sabbath

Children's Sabbath is part of a national advocacy program for children from the Children's Defense Fund. It is celebrated each October and resources can be found at http://www.childrensdefense.org. The following prayer uses songs children (and adults) can learn as responses. This prayer would be appropriate for other services focused on children as well.
The Lord is with you.
And also with you.

Lift up your hearts.
We lift them up to the Lord.
Let us give our thanks and praise.
It is right to give our thanks and praise to God.
We rejoice to give you thanks and praise, Holy God.
You made us and love us and call us to be your children.
Today we remember all your children around the globe.
Help us to live in peace and love with each other.
Guide us to where our presence and help is needed by others.
Thank you for loving us and giving us each other to love.
Sing: God is so good (*traditional*)
You sent Jesus as a child to learn and grow like us.
Jesus reached out to include children.
He taught his disciples
    that they needed to become like children
    to enter the kingdom of God.
Jesus tells us to offer cups of water,
    clothes, food, and care
    whenever we see someone in need.
Jesus gave us this meal to remember him,
    so that whenever we eat bread and drink the cup,
    we might know that he is with us.
Sing: Jesus loves the little children
        (*traditional African American hymn*)
Send your Holy Spirit on us and on this table.
Fill us to do your will and follow your ways.
We thank and praise you, Holy God.
Sing: Spirit of the living God (*Daniel Iverson*)

WEDDINGS

Communion can be a wonderful way to acknowledge the new life that a wedding can bring. Communion in this setting, as in all regular worship settings, needs to include the entire congregation, not just the wedding party. Be clear in the invitation to the Communion service.

It is appropriate to have the wedding couple serve Communion, if they are active in church and comfortable serving by intinction. For ease, give the bride the bread and the groom the cup, so no one will worry about wine or juice stains on a white bridal gown.

Great Thanksgiving for Weddings

This prayer is based on John 2:1-12 and 1 Corinthians 13.

The Lord God be with you.
And also with you.
Let us thank God for this day and all our days.
We rejoice to give our thanks to God.
We do rejoice and give you thanks, Source of all Love.
You made us in your image,
    and called us to live in community with one another.
Even when we break bonds of love and friendship,
    you continue to model for us grace and harmony.
And so with all the company of heaven
        and all creatures on earth,
    we praise your name and join the hymn:
Holy are you, O God, Source of love and life.
Your glory fills the earth and heaven.
Blessed are those who live in your love.
Blessed, too, is Jesus Christ,
        who went with his mother to a wedding in Cana.
When she discovered the family's need,
    Mary called on Jesus to share his gifts.
He turned water into wine,
    just as he continues to turn our ordinary lives
        into extraordinary blessings.
Through his first miracle, Jesus blessed the guests
    at that wedding feast.
Through this feast of bread and cup,
    Christ comes to bless this couple and our gathering.
Through the love of (Name) and (Name), may the Spirit
    spread love into the world.

Come now, Spirit of God,
        and turn these elements into sparkling joy for us,
    that we may reveal your love for the world,
        building community wherever we go.
Build up this couple and all who support them,
    that they and we may model your true community
        for the world.
We give you thanks, loving God. Amen.

Resources for Weddings

Congregational songs for singing during the service
    "As Man and Woman We Were Made" by Brian Wren
    "Jesus, Joy of Our Desiring" by Martin Janus
    "For the Beauty of the Earth" by Folliot S. Pierpoint
    "One Bread, One Body" by John B. Foley

Table dismissals
    • Go in peace and love into the world.
    • Arise, go, and let the world know God's love.
    • Go into the world to build communities of love.

DEATH AND RESURRECTION

Communion is appropriate during funeral or memorial services as we seek comfort from God and recognize that the deceased is now part of the communion of saints. As in weddings, it is important that the invitation make it clear that all are invited, not just members of the family.

Great Thanksgiving for Services of Death and Resurrection

This prayer is based on Romans 8:31-39.
    The Lord be with you.
    And also with you.

Lift up your hearts.
We lift them up to the Lord.
Let us give thanks to the Lord our God.
We give God thanks for the life of (Name).
We are indeed thankful, O God, for the life
    of your servant, *(Name)*,
    and *her/his* presence among us.
You created us and made us to live in communion
    with you and with each other.
This community feels torn now with the death of *(Name)*.
You alone, O God, can mend us into your new community
    with your saints here and those above,
        for you promised that nothing, not even death,
        could separate us from your love in Christ Jesus.
As Jesus faced his own death, he remembered you,
    gave you thanks, and shared a meal
        with his disciples and friends.
In remembering Christ, we remember all whom we love
    who now reside with you in your eternal presence.
Pour out your Spirit on these elements and on us
    that we may feast with Jesus Christ
    and with all those who have departed this life
        to be with you.
Give us your healing love,
    that we may be strengthened in these days.
Through Jesus Christ, with the Holy Spirit,
    all honor and glory is yours, Almighty God,
        now and forever. **Amen.**

Resources for Services of Death and Resurrection

Congregational songs for singing during the service
"Healer of Our Every Ill" by Marty Haugen
"Here Is Bread, Here Is Wine" by Graham Kendrick
"Hymn of Promise" by Natalie Sleeth
"O God, Our Help in Ages Past" by Isaac Watts

"Precious Lord, Take My Hand" by Thomas A. Dorsey
"Stand By Me" by Charles Albert Tindley
"You Are Mine" by David Haas

Table dismissals

- Arise and go, knowing that you are connected at Christ's table with loved ones from all times and places.
- Arise, sustained by the comfort of this holy meal.
- Take this holy sacrament to your comfort.
- Go, remembering that the Good Shepherd is walking beside you.
- Arise, knowing that Jesus Christ has met you and can help you bear this loss.

CHAPTER FOUR

ADDITIONAL RESOURCES

GENERAL INFORMATION ON COMMUNION

For further reading, particularly on the history of Communion, see *Eucharist: Christ's Feast with the Church* by Laurence Hull Stookey (Nashville: Abingdon Press, 1993).

For a more general introduction, see:

- *Sunday Dinner: The Lord's Supper and the Christian Life* by William Willimon (Nashville: Upper Room Books, 1981).
- *The Shape of the Liturgy* by Dom Gregory Dix (Continuum International Publishing Group; Reprint edition, 2000).
- *This Holy Mystery: A United Methodist Understanding of Holy Communion*, adopted by the denomination's General Conference in 2004. This study can be viewed or downloaded from the following Web site: http://www.gbod.org/worship/.

BREAD

For Communion bread recipes, check the following Web sites:

- http://www.upperroom.org/alivenow/2001/julaug/ greatforgroups.asp?week=7
- http://www.holycomfort.org/vtsbread.html

- http://www.luthersem.edu/resources/communion_bread_ recipe.asp
- http://www.breadwithoutborders.com/

JUICE

For more information on the use of grape juice and individual glasses, see:
- *Christian Worship and Technological Change* by Susan J. White (Nashville: Abingdon Press, 1994), pages 80-87.

LEFTOVER ELEMENTS

See "The Distribution of Communion by the Laity to Those Who Cannot Attend Worship" by Laurence Hull Stookey in *Worship Matters: A United Methodist Guide to Ways to Worship, Volume I*, ed. E. Byron Anderson (Nashville: Discipleship Resources, 1999), pages 147-54.

Or see an earlier version at "Appendix One: Extending the Eucharist to the Unwillingly Absent" in *Eucharist: Christ's Feast with the Church*, Laurence Hull Stookey (Nashville: Abingdon Press, 1993), pages 155-59.

COMMUNION VESSELS

For further information, see *United Methodist Altars: A Guide for the Local Church* by Hoyt L. Hickman (Nashville: Abingdon Press, 1984, 1992).

Or, for more information and drawings of vessels and symbols of the church, see *Worship Without Words: The Signs and Symbols of Our Faith* by Patricia S. Klein (Brewster, Mass.: Paraclete Press, 2000).

ADDITIONAL WORSHIP RESOURCES

For additional invitations to Communion, see *Chalice Worship*, ed. Colbert S. Cartwright (St. Louis: Chalice Press, 1997), pages 405-8.

For further information on lectionary readings, see *The Revised Common Lectionary* (Nashville: Abingdon Press, 1992).

DATE DUE

264 Wal

Communion services

_____Property of_____

Rose City Park United Methodist Church

LIBRARY
ROSE CITY PARK
UNITED METHODIST CHURCH
5830 N.E. ALAMEDA
PORTLAND, ORE. 97213